T l

―

"There are only a handful of people you will meet on your life journey who will alter your course in a profoundly positive way. Dominick is one of those people. His years of training and continuous self-development make him highly qualified as a coach, author and speaker. But it is his genuine desire to improve the lives of all those who will listen, which makes him so unique. Listen, and you will be inspired. Do, and your life will be transformed."

LINDA KNOX
HEAD OF INNOVATION LAB, PRUDENTIAL RETIREMENT

"The three themes of Dominick's book are Awakening, Disrupting and Designing – yet this is not the kind of ADD you're used to. You won't experience one second of inattention, hyperactivity or distraction, just a compelling combination of creative graphics and potent pieces of wisdom that are sure to help you creatively design your future."

ROBERT FRIEDMAN
MANAGING DIRECTOR, NATURE'S SECRET NUTRIENT

"After a year in the trenches at the second startup I founded, my team and I were on the brink of burn-out and we needed help. We brought in Dom to help us focus on what really matters, and the results have been extraordinary, both in terms of revenue and profound feelings of satisfaction at work. Dom has an ability to cut through the fog and get to the heart of what produces real results."

MARK KRASSNER
FOUNDER, EXPECTFUL

"As a women leading a movement dedicated to supercharging the superpowers of women through financial literacy, it's so refreshing to find a conscious and heart-centered man who cares deeply about helping women thrive in business. Dominick engaged with our community in such a meaningful way that they've literally begged me to have him come back. This really says it all!"

JENNIFER LOVE
VISIONARY CEO, ONE MORE WOMAN

"Listen to this life design prophet and you will profit! Dominick is a sage source of game-changing wisdom, and a launching pad for life-changing action."

MATTHEW CROSS
CEO, LEADERSHIPALLIANCE.COM;
AUTHOR OF SET YOUR PRIORITIES STRAIGHT

"Inspired, motivated, confident. This is how you leave an interaction with Dominick. He has a unique ability to quickly get to the core of what holds us back from optimal performance in our personal and professional lives. The wisdom he imparts is well beyond his years. I am a much better father, husband, leader and friend because of working with Dominick.

HARRY DALESSIO
HEAD OF US SALES AND STRATEGIC RELATIONSHIPS,
PRUDENTIAL RETIREMENT

"Dominick is the real deal. He has been my business and personal coach, I've attended his men's retreats and I've worked with him in his former life in financial services. Dominick has the unique ability to help high performers step out of the busyness of life to identify the most impactful actions to achieving what you want in life."

PAUL POWELL
FINANCIAL ADVISOR, NFP RETIREMENT

"I've had the pleasure of coaching Dom over the past three years and can say he is thoughtful, authentic and really walks his walk. He is driven to improving the lives of others, giving them the tools to create a life of passion, freedom and meaning. This book has the code to designing a future you can't wait to live into!"

JOHN O'CONNOR
PRESIDENT, GUIDING THE SHIFT

"Dominick's most critical message is to relentlessly accumulate small wins by setting realistic goals with tangible deadlines. Following the small wins approach was key to my success because I built confidence with each win and would move on to the next goal. The results are remarkable. The process led me to de-stress, improve my time management and I got into my best physical shape in 15 years."

BEN TROMBLEY
VP PORTFOLIO MANAGER, GOLDMAN SACHS

DOMINICK QUARTUCCIO

DESIGN YOUR FUTURE

3 Simple Steps to Stop Drifting
and Take Command of Your Life

AWAKENING | DISRUPTING | DESIGNING

Editing by Kelly Irving
kellyirving.com

Cover design and internal layout by Ellie Schroeder
ellieschroeder.com

Published by TCK Publishing
tckpublishing.com

dominickq.com

CONTENTS

PREFACE

Acknowledging that I was emotionless and numb to the life I had created for myself was, I thought, an admission of failure.

I mean, how could I ask for help if I was incapable of helping myself?

These were the thoughts and feelings that snowballed internally throughout 2009.

Yet, ironically, 2009 was also by far the most successful time of my life. I was the youngest sales VP at my Fortune 100 company, I lived in a top-floor corner apartment in Greenwich Village, Manhattan, I'd just finished my MBA at New York University and had celebrated with a lengthy (for corporate America, at least) excursion in South America. That was the year that I tripled my sales goal. Financially speaking, it was the type of year that compensation committees decree, "Well *that's* never happening again."

Despite the professional success, the financial windfall and the social escapades, 2009 was a dark year for me. I felt myself hurtling 120mph down the SHOULD do this, and need MORE and BIGGER that road, only to find myself at the end of the year lost, with my drive stalled and my mojo meter on empty.

So for the first time in my life, I did what I feared most: I asked for help.

Up until that point, I'd held a deep-rooted belief that asking for help meant I was admitting that I had failed. How wrong that proved to be.

I confided in trusted mentors, attended personal development seminars, hired coaches, devoured libraries of books, revamped my information diet, modeled the behaviors of those whose lives I admired, and experimented with mindfulness and other spiritual practices.

Unknowingly, this set me on the very path of awakening, disrupting and ultimately designing a future I couldn't wait to live into.

The next six years became the most exciting, rewarding and transformative years of my life, ultimately culminating in leaving an incredible career in corporate America to pursue the next evolution of my journey: speaking, coaching and training people who live the life that I used to.

You don't need to suffer in silence with feelings of restlessness or being trapped by your success anymore. Nor do you need to leave your job to experience freedom and empowerment. There is another way.

In this book, I unpack and share this process with you. You will learn how to break free from limiting beliefs, stories and behaviors that are operating in your blind spots and simultaneously creating a ceiling over your future. I will teach you how to connect with what matters in your life, so you can design a dynamic and inspiring future.

This is a conscious commitment to being in action around these principles in your daily life. Your old patterns will always be tugging at you to default back to limiting ways of being.

I won't let that happen to you.

I've written this book so you can keep returning to it over and over again as you encounter new circumstances in your life. In the last chapter, you'll learn the importance of sustaining the progress that you've made.

My journey of self-discovery provided some of the most meaningful, challenging and rewarding moments of my life, including wrapping up an incredible 15-year career in financial services and embarking upon a purpose-driven one that's produced this very book in your hands. This is how I got my mojo back. You may get your mojo back be rekindling your love with the work you already do and the relationships you're already in. Everyone's journey is different and personal.

I also want you to know that it's completely outside of my comfort zone to share so much about myself. (I'm sure you can relate to that.) But sharing stories is the key to transformation, which is why you'll find a lot throughout this book, both from me and from my clients.

The people I work with reiterate how much my story illuminates conditions in their own lives that they need to address. So it's in this spirit that I share myself openly with you. I also thank my clients for sharing their stories of transformation.

I am now designing a future I can't wait to live into.

And you can too.

This book will show you how.

INTRODUCTION

"The first principle is that you must not fool yourself, and you are the easiest person to fool."

— RICHARD P. FEYNMAN

I often find myself face-to-face with highly successful people, like you, who can't seem to figure out why they are increasingly restless in the lives they've created for themselves.

On the one hand, you may genuinely enjoy the work you do, you're compensated handsomely, hold an esteemed position in your work and community, and love/are loved by those around you.

Yet on the other hand, you're not interested in the life you've created for yourself. What once excited you, doesn't as much anymore. Your highs aren't all that high, your lows aren't all that low – and you have no idea why.

Other than the occasional frustration or fleeting moment of happiness, you can't escape the feeling *that you're not feeling much at all.*

Yet you still want to protect the life you have.

And life isn't painful enough yet to change.

So you remain ... living ... but into a future of *more of the same.*

Pain is not your enemy.
The real enemy is when you don't
feel much of anything at all.

YOU'RE TRAPPED

Sometimes it's spoken explicitly. Other times, it's lurking back there behind a façade of achievement, a quiet desperation that something is not quite right, you just don't know what.

There's a growing inner restlessness, the source of which eludes (and confounds) you. After all, you have so many reasons to be grateful, why would you ever feel discontent? Unsatisfied? Bored? Stuck? Fearful? Trapped?

Despite your resistance, these unspoken feelings persist.

'Trapped' is what you feel when you are living into a future of more of the same.

It's a death sentence for someone like you. Nothing will extinguish your fire, your drive, or your ambition faster than the idea of living into a *predictable, uninspiring future*.

Predictable, uninspiring futures are often the byproduct of a life lived in a perpetual state of busyness.

Life is moving so quickly that you don't have a moment to catch your breath.

Your work is never done. You finish one thing only to have 20 other things waiting for you. Your inbox taunts you with notifications of mounting unread messages. You've heard of "inbox zero" but know it's really just a fairy tale.

Your responsibilities at home are never done. There's always someone else's needs to take care of. A broken thing to fix; an errand to run; a to-do list that never seems to shrink.

After unloading on everyone else, all you want to do is collapse into a couch and disappear into a stream of Netflix.

I can't tell you how many of my clients have opened up to me in a moment of candor to reveal the same fantasy:

"I wish I could just go live on an island somewhere that no one wants or needs anything from me. I can escape. I can finally relax."

One of my clients said he was ready to trade places with the Tom Hanks character in *Castaway*. All he wanted was to be assured of a couple of coconuts, Wilson (the volleyball and imaginary friend), and complete solitude.

When it takes 110% of what you've got simply to stay on the increasingly faster hamster wheel of life, it's no wonder you feel trapped.

COMMAND NOT CONTROL

On some level, there's a subtle yet taunting belief that you've lost *command* to change your outcome.

I intentionally use the word "command" instead of "control" for a few reasons. Being in command means you retain *ultimate authority* to call the shots in your life without being involved in every minute detail.

Command is the quiet confidence and understanding that there are certain things you cannot control, and you're at peace with that.

Control freaks, however, believe that they must have a hand in every single variable that could affect the outcome they desire.

Now in my experience, most high achievers like you skew towards the end of the control-freak spectrum. You make bad personal and professional decisions when you feel like you're losing control over your circumstances. Yes, raise your hand if you can relate.[1]

I see this all the time with my clients who have been perpetually successful. They've made excellent money, have big titles, constantly assume bigger responsibilities in and out of work. By all accounts they've accumulated an admirable place in life.

1 Weirdo. You're reading a book with your hand raised.

Yet at the same time, the things that once provided the drive – hitting a certain income threshold, running a specific department, leading however many people, climbing yet another mountain – just don't fire them up anymore.

It's confusing, frustrating and in some cases isolating. After all, who would empathize with you when your life looks so enviable from the outside looking in? Your friends would look at you in disdain. Uncle Harold at Thanksgiving would give you the stink eye.

So you continue to suffer in silence.

Trapped.

RIGHT NOW, YOU ARE FACED WITH TWO OPTIONS:

1

Do the SHOULD stuff

You believe that you SHOULD fulfill societal expectations to bring you happiness. "I SHOULD settle down." "I SHOULD be a better colleague at work." "I SHOULD have another kid."

The problem with SHOULD is that those are external inputs, they don't stem from *you*. Doing some of those things may work, may make you happy – for a while. But most of the time they won't do anything, except make you *even more unsatisfied.*

The MORE and BIGGER approach, which can lead to tremendous financial success, is often flawed in the long run. You're still not connected to what matters to you. It's like pouring water into a glass with no bottom.

2

Double down on MORE and BIGGER
You believe that if you did MORE and BIGGER things, then you'd eventually become happy or satisfied. "Maybe MORE responsibility will motivate me." "My trip to Tahoe isn't BIG enough ... but the Swiss Alps will be." "I need to sit on MORE charity boards and double the size of my team to achieve BIGGER revenue growth."

THE THIRD,
AND UNHEARD, OPTION

3

Now that I've held you under water long enough, it's time to bring you up for some air.

There is another way.

What if you could design a future that you couldn't wait to live into?

I'm talking about the kind of future where, when you envision it, there's such a deep, burning sense of excitement to create a reality that it instantly inspires you in this moment, right now.

What if you were *excited* when the alarm went off in the morning, knowing the day had something amazing in store for you? What if that could be your every morning?

What if you could obliterate the "if I only had more time" virus that's infected you and 99.9% of those around you? What if you actually felt you were in command of your time, truly believed you had enough of it and could do precisely what you want to with it?

What if you could free yourself from your own limiting habits and fears? What if other people's expectations and judgments slid off you like Teflon? What if you could walk your own path and not give a shit about what anyone else thinks?

When you can tap into that kind of feeling, it's like taking some kind of limitless pill.

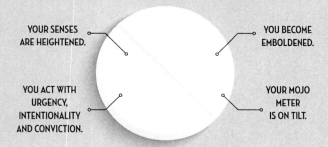

YOUR SENSES ARE HEIGHTENED.

YOU BECOME EMBOLDENED.

YOU ACT WITH URGENCY, INTENTIONALITY AND CONVICTION.

YOUR MOJO METER IS ON TILT.

If you're saying to yourself, "yeah, that *sounds* kind of awesome ..." but you're not wholeheartedly *feeling* the possibility of it just yet, don't worry. At this point, all you need to do is believe that it might just be possible.

I mean, what other option do you have? (Apart from options one and two, which sound shitty, right?).

If you're feeling restless or trapped, which I'd say you are because you're reading this book, then the good news is you're primed to make *meaningful change in your life*.

Believe it or not, you're in a good place.

So just how does this third option work?

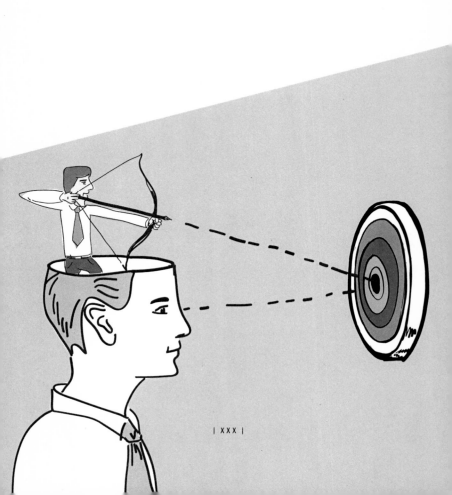

CONSCIOUSLY CREATE YOUR FUTURE

A tremendous number of studies, and Nobel-prize winning research, which we'll explore in this book, have shown that our thoughts, feelings and behaviors are driven automatically by the subconscious. This is what habit is. This is where it lives.

The problem is, you have never consciously designed your habits.

You've just let them happen to you. Therefore, your future is also happening to you. You repeat the same automatic thoughts, feelings and behaviors over and over again. Hence the restlessness, the loss of command, the feelings of being trapped.

There's a way out of this perpetual cycle, a way to take back command of your life and *design a future you can't wait to live into.*

*The process is simple
– but it won't be easy.*

We're talking about rewiring years, often, decades of hardwired behavior. So set your expectations accordingly: this is not a quick-fix solution. Nothing worth attaining in life is quickly attainable. (But, of course, you already know that because that's what got you here in the first place.)

So to set out on this journey – because it will be a journey: a journey of life-changing discovery and of action – you must first understand where you are starting from, from where you're at right now.

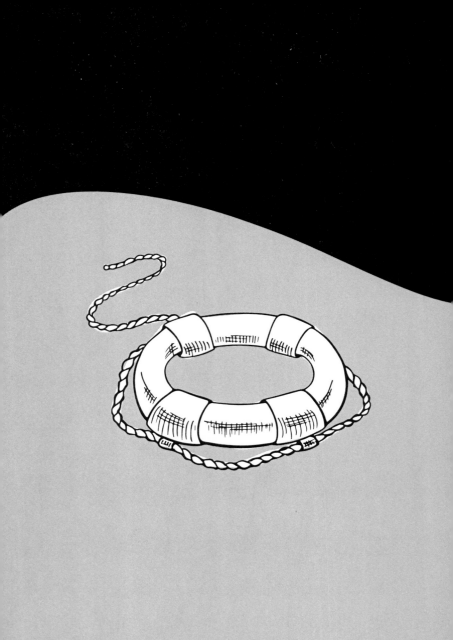

PAST

Are you drifting?
How did you get to this point?

CHAPTER 1

DRIFTING

---

*"People do not decide their futures,
they decide their habits and their
habits decide their futures."*

- F.M. ALEXANDER

When I was eight, in first grade, we used to play this game called Around the World.

The premise was simple: Two kids would stand in front of the first desk. The teacher would read out a math problem like, "what's 6 + 6?" and the first one to answer correctly would move on to challenge the kid sitting at the next desk. If you lost, you had to sit down at the desk of the kid who beat you.

I dominated this game. I loved math and numbers, especially when it came to memorizing the statistics of my favorite baseball players like Don Mattingly (circa '85). I had thousands of baseball cards and could tell you the batting averages of hundreds of players and the present-day stock market trading values of their cards.[2]

So I'd often bulldoze the other kids. Some of my classmates, already resigned to their defeat, would stand up, wait for me to fire out my answer, and obediently sit back down. Nearly every time the game would end without anyone beating me, or even coming close.

What none of the other kids knew, however, was that I grew to *hate* playing this game. In fact, I became terrified of it.

That's because eventually every Mike Tyson meets his Buster Douglas.[3] In first grade, there were two Buster

2   I was slightly obsessive.

3   That was around the same time when Mike Tyson's "Punch Out" came out on Nintendo. It was a formative stage in my life. Stop judging me.

Douglases: Steve and Tim. They were twins, my best friends and my toughest competitors. Early on, I beat them. But then they got better. And eventually, they started beating me.

When I'd lose, I'd be devastated. I felt ashamed. Useless.

Pretty extreme response for a stupid game, right? I see the ridiculousness in it now. But as for most kids this age, *everything* was like life or death: grades, girls, sports, praise from my parents, God's approval of my behavior...

That's why I grew to despise and fear playing Around the World. It was like a microcosm for the rest of my life: Keep winning, and I'll be okay. Lose, and my world would spiral out of control.

Winning felt so fleeting. Failure felt so permanent.

A single loss could wipe out 20 consecutive wins.

On the deepest of *emotional levels*, I only believed I was good when I was performing, behaving "the way I was supposed to" and receiving praise from external sources. Anytime I failed, didn't behave the way others expected or disappointed an authority figure, I felt threatened and rejected.

Sometimes failure or the fear of it would get so bad I'd have cripplingly sharp pains in the pit of my stomach. I was eight years old!

External validation is a fickle and flimsy foundation on which to build a life, yet it starts at such an early age.

I would go on to organize the rest of my childhood, teenage years and adult life around this constant need for external validation.

My guess is, to some degree, that you have done this too.

All of this was predicated on the deepest-rooted belief that I had no inherent value and that only external sources could validate me. *None of this was consciously designed.* It simply happened.

Therefore, my unconscious strategy – and possibly your unconscious strategy – has been to become an expert at attaining external validation.

I mastered social dynamics, became a valuable teammate/employee, learned how to attract women, grew into a leader, crushed goals ... rinse and repeat.

Whatever your external validation has been, like me, the strategy has brought you many spoils: money, status, opportunities, praise, social standing and, most importantly, acceptance.

Yet, the "acceptance" you've attained is, on some level, untrue. It's an acceptance of your façade, not the authentic you. The authentic you is hidden, buried somewhere safe. Protected from the threat of exposure and rejection. This is one of the greatest sources of your dis-ease, and you may have no idea that it's even happening.

This is why when you get to the point of being "on top of the world" years and years later, you experience numbness and disconnection to your on-paper success.

That's because you've been focusing on the outside, of everything external to yourself, and now you're completely out of touch with the inside, of your own internal compass.

I didn't know it at the time, but the only way I could break free from this trap was to address the most fundamental hard-wiring in my operating system: my habits.

My intent is to save you a ton of the trouble, time and effort that I went through to illuminate these elusive little suckers so you can start to understand what habits are driving you.

IT'S NOT WHAT YOU THINK

Biting your nails, quitting smoking or checking Facebook 176 times a day are small games for average people. You're not an average person, so these are not the habits I am talking about.

Designing a future you can't wait to live into is no ordinary feat. It requires you to dig deep below the surface-level stuff and deconstruct the habitualized rubbish that's oppressing your fullest potential (like my need for external validation).

So first we need to re-orient your understanding of what habits are.

Habits manifest in two layers:

1. **Surface level:** your behaviors

2. **Deep level:** your beliefs and stories

It's your beliefs that give rise to the stories you tell yourself, which drive your behaviors, as shown in Figure 1.1.

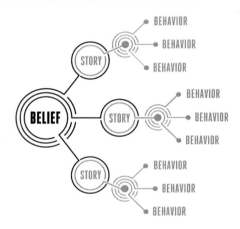

Figure 1.1: Beliefs, stories and behaviors

Let's look at each in more detail.

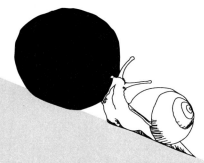

1. Beliefs

This is what you believe to be true, at the deepest core of your being. In many cases, beliefs are not consciously adopted, rather, they are a byproduct of your upbringing, environment and experiences.

Some examples of limiting beliefs:

» I need others to approve of me.

» Money is the root of all evil.

» The world is a dangerous and scary place.

They sound silly, right? These may be words that would never in a million years leave your mouth. But if you were to be 100% honest with yourself about what's driving your behaviors, these may very well be the types of beliefs buried at the root of it all.

2. Stories

Stories are your ongoing internal narrative, that little voice in your head that keeps chattering away about the same things day in and day out. Stories are often unconscious because they stem from your beliefs.

Some examples of stories:

- » Being liked is more important than speaking up for what I truly believe in.

- » I must respect other people's needs before my own.

- » If I get _____ title and make _____ money, then I'll be happy.

Beliefs are the seeds of your habits.
Stories are the roots of your habits.
Behaviors are the sprouts of your habits.

3. Behaviors

Behaviors are the result of your actions, which come from your beliefs and the stories you tell yourself. When people talk about habits, your behavior is most often what they're referring to. Some examples of behaviors:

» Checking my phone incessantly
  in case someone needs me.

» Saying yes to other people's requests,
  even at expense of myself.

» Taking on roles and responsibilities
  that don't inspire me because it brings
  me external praise and closer to the
  threshold where I will finally be happy.

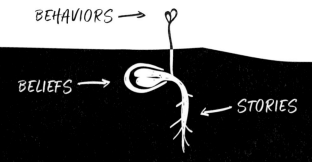

BEHAVIORS →

BELIEFS →

← STORIES

DIGGING BENEATH THE SURFACE

When we talk about habits, 99% of the time we are referring to the surface-level stuff, your behaviors.

Remember, some common behaviors include:

» nail-biting

» overeating at every meal

» checking your phone 174 times a day

» drinking a glass of wine every night

» smoking when stressed.

Why is it that our behavior seems to get all the attention?

Mainly because behavior is visible and tangible.

Yet your actions come from your beliefs and stories, which are *far* more responsible for your behaviors than anything else.

Charles Duhigg's *The Power of Habit* explores the surface-level layer of habits (and does so quite brilliantly).

Duhigg refers to The Habit Loop, which has three stages:

1.   **Cue:** a stimulus

2.   **Routine:** the response

3.   **Reward:** the payoff

For example: I'm hungry and spot a Chipotle (cue), I enter the store and ingest a two-pound burrito (the response), I fall into a deep state of temporary bliss (reward) followed by a slightly less temporary period of self-loathing.[4]

Duhigg goes on to describe a fourth stage, which is the craving that develops after attaining a pleasurable reward. That craving makes you even more susceptible to the cue the next time you encounter it.[5] In turn, The Habit Loop strengthens and you find yourself increasingly beholden to it, unless you break the Loop by altering your response (the routine) to the cue.

---

4   Duhigg provides no guidance on what to do with this sensation.

5   Hence my propensity to hypnotically enter Chipotle establishments without thinking.

While Duhigg's guidance is illuminating and useful on many fronts, I also find it equally lacking when it comes to instigating profound, transformational change. This type of change is necessary to break free from a future that's more of the same and to *design a future you can't wait to live into.*

That's because, as you'll begin to see, the surface level of your habits is no more than the proverbial tip of the iceberg.

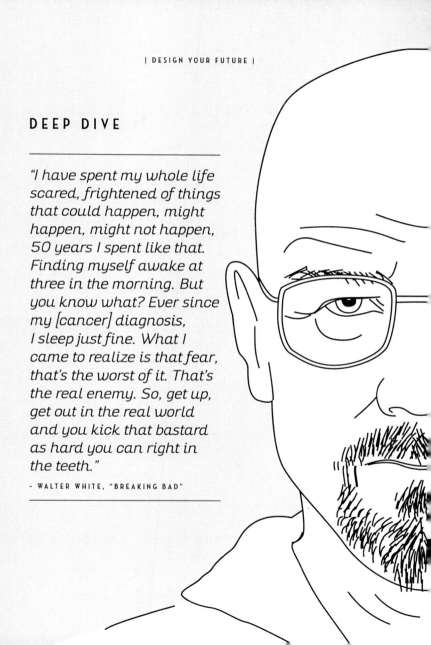

DEEP DIVE

"I have spent my whole life scared, frightened of things that could happen, might happen, might not happen, 50 years I spent like that. Finding myself awake at three in the morning. But you know what? Ever since my [cancer] diagnosis, I sleep just fine. What I came to realize is that fear, that's the worst of it. That's the real enemy. So, get up, get out in the real world and you kick that bastard as hard you can right in the teeth."

- WALTER WHITE, "BREAKING BAD"

In my opinion, "Breaking Bad" is one of the greatest TV series of all time.[6] Walter White, the protagonist, is a lifelong underachiever in his 50s teaching high school chemistry to students. When he's diagnosed with terminal cancer and the prospect of leaving nothing behind to a pregnant wife and a son with cerebral palsy, he realizes he needs to take drastic measures to reverse his dim fate.

White's background in chemistry finally serves a purpose when he links up with one of his former deadbeat students who introduces him to the crystal meth game. As it turns out, White is a chemistry genius, and he soon becomes the best in the world at cooking crystal meth. This, as you can probably imagine, generates a cornucopia of family-friendly television scenarios...

What makes the show so extraordinary, is you get to witness the radical transformation of a resigned, cynical and helpless man into a ferocious, dangerous and wildly arrogant dictator.

As White "breaks bad" he goes from having a fundamental belief that he's an irreconcilable loser to an equally

---

6   Along with "Lost", "The Wire" and "The Sopranos"

powerful belief that he's godlike.[7] When these beliefs change, everything in his life – his stories about himself and his behaviors – change too.

Unfortunately, neither of White's underlying – and polarizing – beliefs were consciously decided by White. (Without ruining the story for you, this lack of consciousness leads to severe consequences for him, his family and everyone who comes into contact with him.[8])

Now, not to insinuate that you're a maniacal, narcissistic meth-chemist on the verge of bringing everyone in your life down, but there are some similarities to be drawn here[9]...

---

7 "I am the one who knocks!" – Walter White

8 But it does make for exceptional television!

9 Hear me out ;-)

BRAIN BLAME

The key insight from Walter White is his utter lack of consciousness of his internal operating system: how his brain works.

Chances are, your understanding could use some work too. Your brain is the ultimate liberator—or oppressor—in your life. The choice is yours which it will be, and it boils down to your understanding of how your brain operates.

This is where we start to unlock the forces that currently work without your conscious approval, yet are responsible for 95% of your life's results.

In his *New York Times* best-selling book *Thinking Fast and Slow*, Nobel Prize winner Daniel Kahneman describes how our mental cognition functions in two systems:

1. **System 1:** Fast, automatic, frequent, emotional, stereotypic, subconscious

2. **System 2:** Slow, effortful, infrequent, logical, calculating, conscious

In other words:

1. **System 1:** Iceberg

2. **System 2:** Tip of the iceberg

As Kahneman says,

> When we think of ourselves, we identify with
> System 2, the conscious, reasoning self that has
> beliefs, makes choices, and decides what to think
> about what to do. Although System 2 believes itself
> to be where the action is, the automatic System 1 is
> the hero ...

Studies cited by Harvard Business School and the US National Library of Medicine highlight that up to 95% of our behavior is dictated by System 1, the unconscious. This is where our belief seeds have been planted, our stories have been sown and our habits sprout.

This is why Walter White, despite the radical transformation in beliefs about himself, is just as trapped in his "powerful" life as he was in his "loser" life – he was unconscious to all of it.

Therefore if you want real transformation, to break free from a future of more of the same and to *design a future you can't wait to live into*, you must begin an expedition into the part of you that's responsible for 95% of your behavior.

This explains why you repeat your patterns over and over again.

The 95% of your operating system that is hiding in your blind spots is churning out all of your habits.

WHAT THE DEVIL IS DRIFTING?

Hurricane Sandy took it easy on me compared to many others in 2012. My Manhattan apartment suffered no damage and was without power, cell service or running water for only five days.

The eerie part, however, was that in Union Square, my neighborhood, it felt like I was living in an episode of "The Walking Dead."[10] Union Square is a vibrant, bustling neighborhood that sees hundreds of thousands of locals and tourists flooding the streets on a daily basis. Yet during Hurricane Sandy, the streets were completely empty. Talk about a pattern interruption.

---

10 Minus the zombies. At least dead ones, that is.

When the sun went down, there was nothing to do other than grab a flashlight and a book. That's when I read the following words, spoken by the Devil in Napoleon Hill's controversial book *Outwitting the Devil*:

> My greatest weapon over human beings is how I gain control of their minds. Habit, through which I silently enter the minds of people. By operating through this principle, I establish the habit of **drifting.** When a person begins to drift, he is headed straight toward the gates of hell.

This passage forever shifted my perspective on how little command I truly owned over my life, and how much I'd unwittingly relinquished to "the Devil."

The Devil is a fictional character that Hill constructed based on 20 years of interviews, observations and insights into some of the world's most successful people at that time (the source material behind his all-time bestselling book *Think and Grow Rich*).

The Devil boasts that 98% of people are under his command, meandering through life in a hypnotic rhythm. Drifting.

---

*"The mind is nothing more than
the sum total of one's habits!"*

- THE DEVIL, OUTWITTING THE DEVIL

So how do you know if you're currently drifting?

THE DRIFT QUIZ

Here's a checklist that I've created from a number of
the drift-identifying characteristics Napoleon Hill
writes about in Outwitting the Devil.

Tick each one you relate to (be truthful now!) and
let's see how you score:

- [ ] You lack purpose in your life.

- [ ] Your fears drive your behavior.

- [ ] You lack enthusiasm and initiative to begin
anything you are not forced to undertake.

- [ ] You're not as magnetic as you would like to be
and you fail to attract other people.

- [ ] You make the same mistakes over
and over again.

- [ ] You begin many things but complete nothing.

- [ ] You eat too much and exercise too little.

- [ ] You criticize others who are succeeding
in your chosen calling.

ARE YOU DRIFTING?

Once upon a time, answering the drift quiz would have felt like one gut punch after another. Lack of major purpose? Guilty. Fear driving my behavior? Guilty. Shaving off parts of my personality to be agreeable and ultimately less magnetic? Guilty.

I'd always convinced myself I was in command of my life. But after reading Hill's book, I realized I was actually a drifter extraordinaire.

As successful as many of my clients are, they'll tell you that by the standards outlined above, they were drifting big time when they first started working with me.

So how do most people break free from drift? Unfortunately, only when an outside force thrusts itself upon them such as:

- » cancer
- » being cheated on
- » losing their job
- » a parent dying
- » when things are so bad they "CAN'T TAKE IT ANYMORE"

Only when you are shaken to your very core (an *awakening*, which we'll explore in the next chapter) do you break free from drift to inspect your underlying operating system.

But this raises a new question:

How in command of your life are you really, if you are dependent on the thrust of an outside force to catalyze change in your life?

STUCK IN STATUS QUO

In my former life in sales, the "status quo bias" was always our toughest competitor.

We rarely feared the competition. Our biggest threat was no change at all: 60% to 80% of our potential opportunities never moved from their existing vendor. In other words, they defaulted towards the status quo.

When you drift, you're stuck in status quo. The status quo is rarely a conscious choice, yet it has Herculean strength.

The status quo is fortified by:

» **Fear of the unknown**
Even when the devil you know is terrible, it hasn't killed you yet. But switching to the devil you don't know *just might*.

» **Switching costs**
I *loathe* Time Warner Cable as my cable provider. I curse them fortnightly.[11] But the thought of going to Verizon and picking up a box, installing it, figuring out a new remote, reprogramming all my DVRs, learning all the new channels ... *God forbid.*

» **Pain of enduring the "same" is less than perceived pain of change**
This is the biggie. Many of my clients are fed up with what they're doing for a living, but the perceived pain of giving up what they've built, starting over or making sacrifices to change course is too great to overcome the current restlessness. So they stay stuck. (We'll look at how you can flip this pain formula in the next chapter.)

When it comes to changing behavior, you don't break from the status quo based on rational thinking. It requires a much deeper internal emotional shift to overcome that 95% default behavior.

---

11 That's a lot.

But the problem – for high-achievers in particular – is that when you think you understand something intellectually, you think your work is done.

But if you know something intellectually, and your behavior doesn't change, then what good is it?

» You may understand intellectually that smoking will kill you. **But you keep puffing.**

» You may understand intellectually that your work-life balance is killing you. **But you keep working.**

» You may understand intellectually that cheating on your partner and your growing porn habit are problematic. **But you keep on philandering.**

Stephen Covey punctuates this point:

"to know and not to do, is not to know."

Simply knowing something intellectually doesn't break you free from drift. In fact, it can force you deeper into status quo, because you've fooled yourself into believing you have the answers.

That is why it's time to break free from drift.

TAKE COMMAND NOW

Command of your life is totally within your grasp. I know it because I changed my life, and I've seen my clients transform theirs through the same process.

You can harness the power of the 95% of your operating system and install a system of habits that will design a *future you can't wait to live into.*

How?

Through the three-step ADD Cycle, as shown in Figure 1.2:

1. Awakening
2. Disrupting
3. Designing

Figure 1.2: The ADD cycle

1. Awakening

Awakening is when you are ready to take action and make change. Awakenings occur through the cultivation of awareness. You cannot change what you are not aware of. The first stage is to uncover the habits that are operating in your blind spots. Once your habits are brought out into the light, you can inspect them, trace their origins and disrupt them.

2. Disrupting

Disrupting is the process of interrupting your perpetual patterns and breaking the stimulus and response cycle. When you do this, you get immediate and profound feedback on why you do what you do, and how these habits may be serving or oppressing you.

3. Designing

Once you've awakened to and disrupted your habits, you've broken the cycle. You've created space between stimulus and response. You can now consciously design new habits that empower your future.

This is your process for breaking free from drift. For abolishing the future of *more of the same* and opening a gateway to *a future you can't wait to live into.*

PRESENT

*It's time to take command
and start living.*

CHAPTER 2

AWAKENING

---

*There are these two young fish swimming along,
and they happen to meet an older fish swimming
the other way, who nods at them and says,
"Morning, boys, how's the water?"
And the two young fish swim on for a bit, and
then eventually one of them looks over at the
other and goes, "What the hell is water?"*

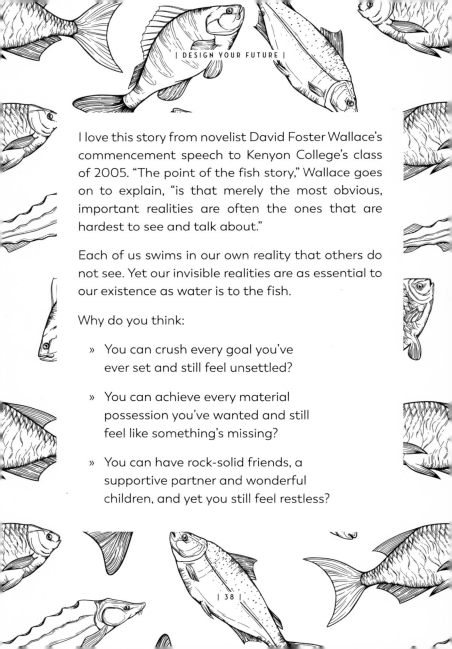

I love this story from novelist David Foster Wallace's commencement speech to Kenyon College's class of 2005. "The point of the fish story," Wallace goes on to explain, "is that merely the most obvious, important realities are often the ones that are hardest to see and talk about."

Each of us swims in our own reality that others do not see. Yet our invisible realities are as essential to our existence as water is to the fish.

Why do you think:

» You can crush every goal you've ever set and still feel unsettled?

» You can achieve every material possession you've wanted and still feel like something's missing?

» You can have rock-solid friends, a supportive partner and wonderful children, and yet you still feel restless?

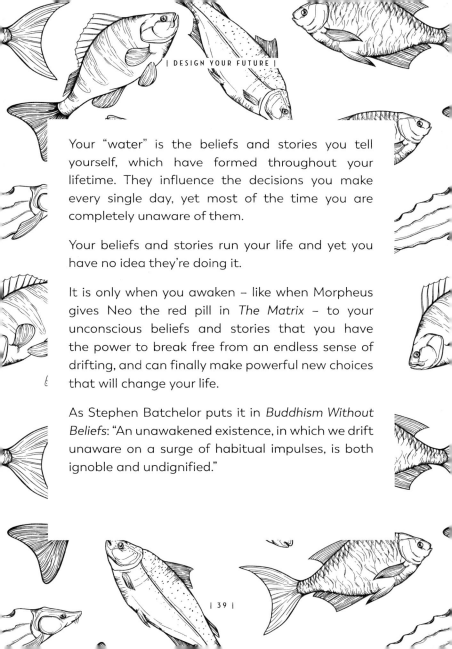

Your "water" is the beliefs and stories you tell yourself, which have formed throughout your lifetime. They influence the decisions you make every single day, yet most of the time you are completely unaware of them.

Your beliefs and stories run your life and yet you have no idea they're doing it.

It is only when you awaken – like when Morpheus gives Neo the red pill in *The Matrix* – to your unconscious beliefs and stories that you have the power to break free from an endless sense of drifting, and can finally make powerful new choices that will change your life.

As Stephen Batchelor puts it in *Buddhism Without Beliefs*: "An unawakened existence, in which we drift unaware on a surge of habitual impulses, is both ignoble and undignified."

If you read this and believe, vehemently, that you're awakened to everything that is going on around you, then that is proof you are the most asleep of all...

You can spend an entire lifetime in an unawakened pursuit of goals, titles, social approval that only pushes you further into a state of quiet desperation and a life of more of the same.

GET REAL

An *awakening* is a moment when something inside of you shifts and creates a monumental external transformation. It means:

you're ready to make a change.

Do you realize *how hard* it is to arrive at this place? Remember 95% of your behavior is automatic and unconscious. As a human, you do everything to resist change.

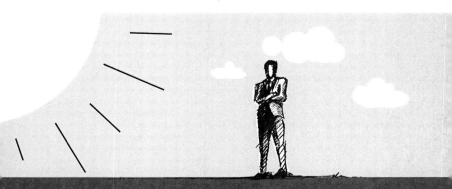

If you've ever seen the documentary *Escape Fire: The Fight to Rescue American Healthcare,* then you'll know what I mean. Roy Litten is a patient in the ER who has had several heart attacks and a stent placed in his heart, but continues to eat eggs and bacon, and to smoke. When Roy's doctor tells him it's time to modify his diet, Roy responds by saying, "Well, I don't want to change my diet until things start to get really bad."

As if you need more evidence that it's time to change than, say, a heart attack.

Alcoholics and drug addicts know that they're killing themselves, and yet tragically some still can't bring themselves to change.

Change is HARD.

That's why an awakening requires you to surrender.

A true awakening must overpower 95% of your unconscious behavior.

So let's talk about what stands in the way of you having an awakening.

THE PAIN-OF-CHANGE EQUATION

In March of 2016, I did my first ten-day silent meditation retreat on the magical Big Island of Hawaii. No talking, no eye contact, no reading, no writing, no exercise ... just pure inward reflection and observing thoughts and feelings for 18 waking hours a day. Heaven or hell?

For one hour each evening, we'd watch a video by the sage S.N. Goenka. On the third day, he provided a profound metaphor for why intellectual understanding gets in the way of so many people's ability to change.

Goenka says that intellectual understanding is like "the leaves on the branches of a tree." Flimsy, constantly changing, easily blown away by the wind. But the trunk and the roots of the tree are the foundation, the strength. This is where existential understanding resides. Unless you understand something existentially, the trunk and roots of your metaphorical tree, change won't happen.

We are hardwired to react to threats instead of responding to rewards, so your most dominant catalyst for change is transforming this equation:

$$\frac{\text{PAIN OF CHANGE} > \text{PAIN OF SAME}}{\text{PAIN OF CHANGE} < \text{PAIN OF SAME}}$$

TO

Once you can flip that pain/same pain/change equation, you're now ready to create lasting change.

So how do we make "the pain of same" greater than the "pain of change?"

Well, first you need to understand the distinction between two types of awakenings:

1. Unintentional

2. Intentional

1. Unintentional awakenings

This is when an outside force thrusts itself upon you, shaking you to your core. A heart attack (unless you're Roy Litten), a job loss, or the loss of a loved one, for example.

As Napoleon Hill's Devil in *Outwitting the Devil* espouses, 98% of the population relies exclusively on unintentional awakenings to make any meaningful change. These forces can be positive or negative experiences.

Seemingly, it's the negative experiences that shake us deeper, harder and more often. Eckhart Tolle, author of the *New York Times* bestseller *The Power of Now* gives us superb advice in these situations:

> Whenever any kind of disaster strikes, or something goes seriously "wrong" – illness, disability, loss of home, or fortune or of a socially defined identity, breakup of a close relationship, death or suffering of a loved one, or your own impending death – know that there is another side to it, that you are just one step away from something incredible: a complete alchemical transmutation of the base metal pain and suffering into gold. This one step is called surrender.

You cannot, nor should you want to, avoid unintentional awakenings. The world is in a constant state of chaos.

Life will come at you in ways that you want, and don't want. As Tolle explains, you can become The Alchemist and gain the power of transforming metal into gold.

2. Intentional awakenings

Very few of us are aware that we have the power to catalyze our own awakening. There's a prevailing and misguided belief that the impetus for real change resides outside of ourselves.

This is a dangerous and faulty assumption, and it's certainly no way to live your life.

Intentional awakenings allow you to illuminate the beliefs, stories and behaviors that were once hidden in your blind spots. Now that you've called them out into the light, you can inspect whether they are serving you or oppressing you.

Better yet, once you've built the habit around creating your own intentional awakenings, you can even turn unintentional awakenings into intentional awakenings. That's why, from this point on, I'm going to guide you to create your own intentional awakening.

WAKE THE HELL UP!

Anyone who routinely catalyzes real change in their lives, without being dependent on an outside force or waiting for insurmountable pain, is going to be the winner of the future.

They win freedom, peace of mind, money, empowerment, greater opportunities, admiration and respect. Best of all, they will design a life they can't wait to live into.

Are YOU interested in these spoils?

You need to focus on ONE thing: cultivating awareness.

You cannot change what you're unaware of. Remember the fish that's unaware of the existence of water? That's you right now.

But if you were to become aware of the water, and understand its properties and effects on your entire reality, then a whole universe of possibilities will open up to you.

Cultivating awareness – your ability to consciously observe what's going on in and around you – is your gateway to consistently creating intentional awakenings in your life.

There are a few ways to put your awareness abilities on steroids. I'm going to share with you five prescriptive methods for cultivating awareness:

1. Examine your beliefs and stories

2. Identify the consequences of the status quo

3. Meditate

4. Hire a coach

5. Attend group personal development seminars

I've personally used each of these methods to cultivate awareness and accelerate awakenings in my life, and they are the foundation for when I coach and train others. So let's look at each now.

1. Examine your beliefs and stories

As discussed in chapter one, your beliefs are the seeds that sow the stories you tell yourself, and the stories you tell yourself sprout the habits and behaviors that determine how your life unfolds.

So if you want real change, you need to go to the root of your problem: your beliefs and stories.

Your beliefs and stories are currently invisible to you. Yet they control your GPS navigation system.

So how do you create intentional awakenings so that you can bring your beliefs and stories out of your blind spots and into your awareness?

Spend some time walking through the following
five steps:

i. Listen to your inner narrative

Without judgment, take inventory of the voice in your
head and what it's saying about your life. How about
"you're not doing enough," or "you shouldn't be sitting
around with so much to do," or "you can't do that, it'd be
too selfish." Snag some of these greatest hits and write
them down. Inspect them. Interrogate them. Figure out
where they came from and whether they are serving you
... or beating you into the ground.

ii. Identify what you fear losing the most

If you lost your job, your family, your lover, your money, your looks, your wit, your humor, or your social standing, then who would you be? The thing you fear losing the most provides excellent cues as to what underpins some of your deepest held beliefs. Is that fear justified?

iii. Inspect your "identity" attachments

"I'm an extreme introvert because Myers Briggs told me so," therefore you increasingly avoid any mildly uncomfortable social setting because of an arbitrary test. Or you're an extrovert and you do the opposite for the same reasons. Maybe someone somewhere along the way called you a brat, an asshole or a genius, and you believed it. Maybe it's time to see if those labels are still relevant.

iv. Recall shitty events

Go back to a particularly painful moment in your childhood or teenage years. You know, like that time you had to give a class presentation and you fumbled, stuttered, or forgot your words in front of everyone. In that moment, you created a story, "I suck at presenting in front of large groups," and you've built a life around a singular moment. Sure, you may have other evidence to support it, but chances are much of that flowed from your original story. What would happen if you chose a new story?

v. Use the five-year-old technique: keep asking "why?"
I know, this one is unoriginal and overplayed, but it's effective. If you've identified something about yourself and you can't figure out why it's there, keep asking "why" until you get to the root cause.

STORY HOTSPOTS

There are several themes, or common beliefs and stories, that it's likely you are telling yourself.

- **Achievement:** You have an incessant need to always be achieving, conquering, checking off boxes. In the absence of achievement you may experience feelings of restlessness, emptiness or even worthlessness.

  "I haven't done anything productive all day and I feel guilty (even though it's Saturday)."

- **External validation:** You need approval from others to experience feelings of worth, value and acceptance. You bask in the glow of external approval. You're terrified of rejection, looking bad or being ostracized. You find yourself doing and saying things that don't agree with you, simply to obtain the security of external validation.

  "Staying out late and drinking at work functions is exhausting, but I don't want everyone else to think I'm lame, so instead I'll just show up hung over and miserable tomorrow."

- **Time:** You never have enough. You're always racing around from one thing to the next, barely making it or you're perpetually late. You say things like "I wish I had more time," and "I'll get to it when I have more time," but you never do. You've thought about doing things for years, but never seem to get around to doing them because you never have enough time.

"I'll eventually look into personal development programs and get back to traveling around the world when I have more time."

For more examples, download "20 places to look for limiting beliefs and stories" from dominickq.com/resources

2. Identify the consequences of the status quo

Studies cited by Harvard Business Review – and conducted by Hal Hershfield of UCLA School of Management – show that our brains are wired in such a way that we have a hard time relating to our future selves.

In fact, fMRI scans of our brain show that we perceive our future selves much in the same way as we do strangers: you don't associate with that person on an emotional level.

You keep screwing your future self over because right now, in this moment, you simply aren't connected to that future version of you.

To overcome this shortcoming of the brain, you need to get crafty.

Your tool here is time travel. No seriously. Stay with me.

We'll use time travel to get you crystal clear on the consequences of staying in status quo.

It's a tremendous fulcrum for flipping the pain-of-change equation:

$$\frac{\text{PAIN OF CHANGE} > \text{PAIN OF SAME}}{\text{PAIN OF CHANGE} < \text{PAIN OF SAME}}$$

To understand this, let's look at one of my clients, Chris. Chris is a medical device sales manager suffocating under 12-hour workdays and six day workweeks with no end in sight, yet he couldn't bring himself to make meaningful changes because he was afraid of backlash from senior management, his boss and colleagues. Besides, he'd survived up to this point, so he'd proved he could endure it.

But what he hadn't fully internalized – because he was so damn stuck – was understanding how staying on this course was affecting the Chris of one year from now ... three years from now ... five years from now ... and a lifetime from now.

"Somebody once told me the definition of hell: on your last day on Earth, the person you became will meet the person you could have become."

- ANONYMOUS

So I asked Chris to spend time reflecting, visualizing and projecting what his life would be like if everything were to continue on the same course:

> Pretend we've just hopped in my time machine[12] and it's exactly one year from today. NOTHING has changed. You've continued working 12-hour days, six days a week for the past 365 days. You've been unable to set boundaries. You've been disempowered for another year.

---

12 "You built a time machine, out of a Delorean?"

- » How do you feel, after another year of living like this?

- » How's your confidence?

- » How's your dating life?

- » How's your attitude?

- » How's your outlook for the next year, and the years beyond it?

When Chris got super clear on the reality he was creating for himself longer term, it started to scare the shit out of him.

Suddenly, he was aware and could the feel pain of a future version of himself he never wanted to become. He borrowed all that future pain and collapsed it into right now. Ultimately, he used it to catalyze an awakening.

Soon enough, the pain-of-change equation flipped.

FLIP THE PAIN-OF-CHANGE EQUATION

Identify the consequences of staying as you are right now, in the status quo:

1. Pick the thing you want, or the thing you want to change.

2. Fast-forward one year into the future, write down the projected date.

3. Pretend you are living in that future moment, as if 365 days are now behind you and you haven't achieved or changed that thing you wanted.

4. Ask yourself how it feels knowing another 365 days have slipped away without any change?

5. Outline the thoughts and feelings you have as a result of staying in the status quo.

6. Project forward another year of no change ... another 365 days of *more of the same*. Record your thoughts and feelings.

Once you've gone through this exercise, you'll end up in one of two places:

1. You can live with **more of the same.**

2. You had an awakening, and you need to get your ass in gear.

Proceed accordingly.

3. Meditate

If I could offer you a pill that provided the following results, would you take it?

- » increased capacity for awareness, concentration and decision making

- » diminished feelings of pain

- » reduced feelings of fear

- » reduced anxiety and depression

- » increased creativity

Sorry to tell you this, but they aren't results, they are *superpowers*.

But what if I told you that you didn't need to ingest anything, and what I'm offering doesn't cost you a dime?

Meditation is free and provides all of the aforementioned benefits. And counter to what you might believe, it's not some hippy or mystic woo-woo shit. This is the tool of titans of past, present and especially the future.

Now, I won't be able to do meditation the justice it deserves in a subsection of a chapter in my humble little book. There are many beautiful books already written about the practice of cultivating mindfulness, and that's why I've listed some of my favorites in the resources section at the end of the book, and also created an online library for you.

What I aspire to do here, however, is to ignite a personal curiosity so that you pursue a meditation practice of your own.

For additional reading and videos on meditation and more, check out Resources on page 189.

Space between stimulus and response

There is a saying (often attributed to Viktor Frankl): "Between stimulus and response there is a space. In that space is our power to choose our response. In our response lies our growth and our freedom."

So how do we access that space between stimulus and response, where our ability to choose resides?

Meditation.

If you want to break your stimulus-response patterns...

If you want to bring your unconscious behaviors out from your blind spots and into the light...

If you want to illuminate the limiting beliefs and stories you've built a life around...

Then meditation is not optional. It's essential.

Meditation slows things down so we can see more clearly. Picture the speed of your mind like a freight train blowing through an intersection at 80 mph. It's going so fast you can barely see the space between the cargo cars. That's like the speed of your thoughts. Meditation allows you to slow things down, so you can actually see the space between the freight train cars ... and have a look at what's on the other side.

Every major intentional awakening I've had over the last five years either happened during, or could be traced back to, my mindfulness practice.

HERE'S A PERSONAL EXAMPLE:

In late 2013, while meditating, I felt a surge of energy around a life-changing possibility, to leave my high-paying corporate gig and become a coach and public speaker.

My whole body was *vibrating*. I'd never felt that before, and the sheer power of the vibration was so foreign – and exciting.

You might think that was the impetus for my transformation. You'd be wrong.

Because the very next thing that followed that powerful feeling was, "You could never make as much money doing that as you are right now."

A bucket of ice water on the flames of possibility that my mind graciously served up.

For whatever reason, I immediately believed that story. Unquestioning. So just like that, the vibrations vanished. The energy evaporated.

Six months rolled off the calendar and I'd done nothing – taken no actions or put anything into motion regarding building a new career. I'd believed that story, hook, line and sinker, and it paralyzed my actions.

It wasn't until another meditation session in February of 2014 when I revisited the idea of launching an entrepreneurial career. The power and resonance of that vibration came back full force.

But so did the voice, "You could never make as much money doing that as you are now."

Except this time, something changed. My practice was stronger now. So I was aware that this was simply a story my mind had served up. Just one story out of an infinite number of stories I could choose to believe. So why did I choose to believe this one without giving it a second thought?

Once I was awakened to the fact that I'd unconsciously adopted a disempowering story, my mind started serving up alterative stories. One of them changed my life: "What if you could make ten times as much in this new world as you are right now? Then what would stop you?"

And in that moment, my entire future was rewritten.

In that moment, I had no clear path to how I could produce ten times as much as I was earning. I didn't necessarily believe it was possible either. But the simple willingness to try on this new story – like you'd try on a pair of jeans to see if they fit – changed everything.

In the days and weeks following, an incredible number of ideas came to me – creative ways that I could blow the financial lid off what I was presently earning. I came up with original ideas, but I also started finding evidence of others who were already doing what I aspired to do … people who were in fact making ten times as much as I was.

As soon as money was no longer a concern, I vowed that February 2016 would be my exit date.

As it turned out, February 26th, 2016 was the last of my 5,370 consecutive days at my employer.

FOUR MEDITATION MYTHS

If you've never meditated before, chances are you have one of these four objections:

1. You can't sit still.

That's ok. Almost everyone who tries meditation for the first time experiences the same challenge. You can start by trying it for just three minutes. Then try to sit still a little longer the next time. As you gradually increase your time spent meditating with each session, you'll notice it gets easier and easier to sit still.

2. You can't clear your mind.

Meditation is about observing, not clearing your mind of all thoughts or experiences. Your mind, by its very nature, is designed to produce thoughts, the same way your heart's job is to beat. Instead of trying to change the nature of your mind, learn to embrace and accept it. Meditation allows you simply to observe your mind, and when you find yourself lost in a thought pattern, the simple act of becoming aware that you've drifted builds your meditation muscle.

3. You can't "do it right."

Of course, a high-achieving perfectionist like you is going to say this. But guess what? You can't fail at meditation. One of the key tenets of meditation is to "observe without judgment." This means you observe and take inventory of whatever is going on, without labeling if you're doing it right or wrong.

4. You're unclear of what impact meditation will have on your life.

Meditation isn't like going on a diet. You can't measure the benefits on a scale. It's a very personal experience. You might meditate consistently for a few days or even weeks without being able to pinpoint exactly what benefit you're experiencing. You are, however, sowing the seeds of enhancing your attention, presence of mind, reducing fear responses and elevating all aspects of your awareness. Just try it and see.

4. Hire a coach

Sure, this sounds a little self-serving because I am a coach. But hear me out.

You're too close to your own shit to even see a fraction of the 95% of your subconscious thoughts and behaviors that are running your life. You need an outside perspective. Someone who isn't so caught up in your tightly held beliefs and stories that are building that cement ceiling over your head.

Good coaching is like equipping you with the most powerful flashlight and biggest magnifying lens in the world to illuminate what operates in your blind spots.

Good coaching can help you identify those limiting beliefs and stories that you can't always get to on your own. It can also help you fully internalize the pain of staying stuck in the status quo.

Good coaching accelerates change in weeks and days that otherwise would take months, years, or even a lifetime.

Most people have never experienced having a captive audience of one: having a person there who is solely focused on you, holding space for you, committed to serving YOU. But for those who have experienced that kind of support, you understand how life changing and powerful it can be.

I've had three formal coaches over the last 15 years. I had the same coach for over 3 years, John O'Connor from Guiding the Shift. We met three to four times each month, and I never could've navigated the transition from corporate professional to entrepreneur without him.

If you've never had a coach before, chances are your biggest fears are picking the wrong person and spending a shitload of money before figuring that out. So here's how you overcome that:

i. **Ask the coach what he/she specializes in**
   If you hear things like "I work to understand your situation and then we'll develop a program tailored to your needs," RUN. You want someone

who specializes in working with specific types of people (like you) with specific types of problems (like yours) and they have a proven process to navigate their clients through change.

For example, I work with financially and socially successful professionals who feel a growing restlessness in their lives. They want to design a future they are excited to live into, and I have a process for helping them do that. I'm not here to fix relationships, help someone build their resume or heal a childhood trauma. I'm clear on that.

ii. **Ask whether he/she has a coach themselves**
If the person you're considering as a coach doesn't have a coach ... RUN. Why would you go to someone who isn't investing in the very service that they are providing for others? This demonstrates they don't value coaching, *so why should you value their coaching?*

iii. Ask what personal development programs they've invested in recently

Your ideal coach should be a continuous learner. They should be constantly raising their game and adding new teaching tools to their arsenal, if they are not ... RUN. If they have to reach back several years for their last personal development program, then they've been out of the game for too long. This means they are stuck somewhere in their lives, and that's going to show up in their coaching of you. You deserve better.

iv. Ask for testimonials

This one isn't rocket science, but you want to hear from at least one or two of their clients who have experienced benefits you're looking to achieve. Don't just ask for any reference; ask for examples that relate to your situation. If those clients aren't rabid fans ... if they don't bowl you over with their enthusiasm for the coach ... RUN.

5. Attend group personal development seminars

Awakening experiences are catalyzed when in the presence of others who are also committed to creating self-induced awakenings.

I cannot overstate the transformative and lasting power of immersive personal development experiences with other people who are on a similar journey.

When I say "immersive," I mean leaving your typical environment and fully committing to a professionally facilitated learning environment for a few days.

You'll find yourself surrounded by others who have made the same commitment you have, and the collective intention and energy supercharges your awakening.

When you experience these types of transformative group experiences, it's like the neuro-networks in your mind and body are having a 4th of July party all weekend long.

But there are tips and tricks you can use to optimize your group personal development experience:

i. **Stop overthinking it**

One of my favorite business and personal development icons, Tom Bilyeu (founder of those Quest nutrition bars you see everywhere) says "I'd rather run a million miles an hour in the wrong direction than ten miles an hour in the right direction."

What he means is that taking action gives you immediate feedback. Either it's the right action and you keep going ... or it was the wrong action, and you'll learn invaluable information for the next attempt. I see so many people sit on the sidelines and debate, "think about," and endlessly search for the perfect program. Get off your ass and get on with it already.

ii. **Seek discomfort**

If it's easy for you to sign up for something, then you're playing too small of a game. You need to feel the price tag. You need to feel the time commitment. You need to feel the "I don't know if I can do this." On the other side of that is incalculable growth, and a tremendous sense of "I can do anything."

iii. Go away

Immersive experiences should take you out of your everyday environment and routine. Disrupting your patterns is critical when it comes to behavior change.

For six years I went to an entrepreneurial training program in Chicago called Strategic Coach. Every three months I had to leave New York, pack away my life for a few days and get on a flight to Chicago. That allowed me to fully commit to the experience, and the airtime facilitated the integration of all the new stuff I learned.

The poor guys who drove in from the Chicago suburbs and went right back home to their families never got the same integration period. They were always the ones who never seemed to change much and who dropped out of the program most quickly. So get out of your environment. Break your patterns. Integrate what you've learned.

iv. Book it now

Some people have the luxury of saying, "I'm doing this next weekend." Chances are your schedule isn't that forgiving. In that case, find a program that speaks to you, pick the soonest available date on your calendar, and BOOK IT.

As soon as you commit to something, your personal development experience has already begun. Mentally and emotionally you're already preparing for it, and you reap the benefits of that. It's the same principle as scheduling a vacation – the day you book it is actually one of the most exciting days of the vacation.

What works for one ...

... does not work for another. Some of the strategies I have just shared will resonate with you, and some will not. I recommend you hone in on the suggestion that you seem to be resisting most.

Resistance is typically a guise for fear, which ironically is telling you this is the action you need to take.

Remember, breaking free from drift isn't easy. You must commit to taking action and be willing to get a little messy in the process of creating self-induced awakenings.

If you really want to change (and because you've read this far I know you do), it's time to wake up and give it a go.

FAILURE IS SUCCESS

One of my clients, Chris, was a wildly successful sales manager for a surgical device company. He came to me because his job was killing him. He routinely worked 12-hour days, six days a week. He was 35 years old, single, with no time or energy for a social or dating life. When he finally got downtime, he was so exhausted that his strategy was to disappear from the world until it was time to go back to work. To use his words, "I couldn't see any light at the end of the tunnel."

On one level, he'd already had an awakening: "I can't do this alone," which is what brought him to hire me. But I soon found out this awakening wasn't deep enough for the kind of change Chris needed.

Within the first few weeks of working with Chris, I realized that while he was in a shitty situation, he was still reluctant to make anything other than minor behavioral shifts out of fear of "rocking the boat" at work. Given his increasing misery and total lack of empowerment in the job, minor shifts weren't going to cut it.

So my job became twofold:

1. Help him find solutions to empower himself and if that failed ...

2. Make him feel how truly disempowered he was so he'd be forced to make the tough decisions he'd be avoiding.

We started designing experiments for him to deploy... experiments that made him uncomfortable ... with the intent of him taking his power back. One experiment was to lay down boundaries with his boss, another was to put his foot down on a managerial conference call, another was to re-establish a long-lost workout regimen.

Each one of these experiments ... failed.

He simply couldn't take his power back. He continued to be steamrolled by work commitments and after a week he gave up on his workout routine because he didn't have the time or energy.

But they also succeeded spectacularly.

With each "failed" experiment, Chris began to awaken to how, at the deepest of levels, he had fully relinquished his power to everyone and everything outside of himself. He had no say in his present or future state. He was at the mercy of his external circumstances, relationships and environment.

When I asked him to meditate on the consequences of not changing and continuing to live into that misery one year, three years, five years from now … he finally had enough.

So, one day, Chris called me. "Dom, I'm ready. It's time to leave." It was like he was a totally different person. I barely recognized his voice. But that's because I'd never met that version of him before. He had taken his power back, thanks to the "failed" experiments that succeeded spectacularly.

Chris finally felt the gravity of the pain he was experiencing, and suddenly the pain of change was no longer as intimidating. Once that shifted, he was ready for change.

How did this play out?

When Chris put in his notice, he informed his employer that he'd be embarking on a travel sabbatical around the world. His company valued him so much that they countered with a five-month sabbatical, retained his equity, and offered him the job of his dreams – running an international sales division – which, of course, he took. How about THAT as a case for making change?

CHAPTER 3

DISRUPTING

"Nothing changes, if nothing changes."

Imagine your life as a train rolling along a railroad track.

When you hit a certain intersection, there's a lever that's stuck in the same position, so your train always veers off in the same direction. You go the same way, see the same things, and experience the same feelings.

More of the same.

You realize your only chance of venturing out into new terrain is to pull the lever. That's scary, because no matter how bored you are traveling the same strip of track, at least you know what you're getting. It's safe, practical and predictable – even if it's slowly eroding your life force.

Now imagine that you've summoned the courage to flip that switch and disrupt that trajectory. Who knows where that new track could take you? The possibilities are limitless.

But that lever has been stuck in place for quite some time, so it'll take real effort to move it. And you better believe it'll want to snap back to its old position as soon as you let go, as soon as you ease back your effort.

This is what it takes to disrupt your habits, your patterns of behavior. You've got to pull the lever, change your course of direction, and take the train off the familiar track.

Who knows where you'll end up? But you've finally opened the horizon to explore new frontiers, to broaden your perspective, to get a better understanding of where you want to head next.

No matter how you're feeling about where you're heading, soon enough you'll come to another intersection, another lever and another choice.

That is the journey of life. Disrupting your patterns is essential if you ever intend to design a life you want to live into.

As motivational guru Tony Robbins (and many others) have said:

"If you do what you've always done, you'll get what you've always gotten."

NEXT STOP: DISRUPTING

In order for us to awaken, we need an answer to the question "why change?"

Disrupting is how we generate deeper insights into *what and how we should change.*

Since 95% of how you think, feel and act is automatic, there is no shortage of disruption opportunities. Here are four examples of awakenings waiting to be disrupted:

1. You realize the reason why you're restless in your life is because you followed the vision your parents set out for you, instead of your own, and your contempt for this life is no longer acceptable.

2. You operate in a perpetual state of busyness, always telling yourself "this is how it is," and "it'll slow down someday." Yet "how it is" is no longer

sustainable and you realize nothing will ever slow down unless you take command.

3. You dive into porn every time you're stressed, under-stimulated or encounter a complex task, leaving you numb, disconnected and without energy when it comes time to be intimate with your partner.

4. You're aware that the only reason you keep saying yes to backbreaking work is because you're afraid of being perceived as someone who can't handle the workload. Fear is driving your decisions. And these decisions are starting to kill your relationship with your family.

These awakenings prime you to take action. However, it is not always clear what the appropriate course of action is long-term. Especially when you've been doing things in a certain way for years, decades or an entire lifetime.

Let me take the pressure off of you: You don't have to figure it all out right now. You simply need to disrupt your patterns.

THREE SIMPLE STEPS

There are three ways to disrupt your patterns, limiting beliefs and behaviors.

1. **Interrupt:** pause or stop

2. **Declutter:** reduce or remove

3. **Experiment:** add or test

Let's walk through each in detail.

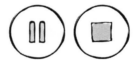

1. Interrupt (pause/stop)

You may think you know why you go to that glass of wine every single night: to "wind down." But take that glass of wine away for 30 days, and I guarantee you you'll find five other deeper reasons – the *real reasons* – why that glass of wine has become a habit. The only way to find out is by interrupting the pattern, or to ...

Change your routine

Let's revisit Charles Duhigg's Habit Loop from *The Power of Habit*.

There are three stages to the Habit Loop:

   i. Cue: a stimulus

   ii. Routine: the response

   iii. Reward: the payoff

For example:

   i. Cue: 3:00pm on a workday and you're tired and bored.

   ii. Routine: A "quick social media scroll" which turns into 25 minutes of phone surfing.

   iii. Reward: Temporary escape from boredom.

While there's most certainly a reward involved, you're not likely to be refreshed nor were you looking to burn 25 minutes reviewing other people's lunches, lattes and (not-so) inspirational quotes.

Duhigg recommends keeping the reward but changing the routine. This would look like:

i. **Cue:** 3:00pm on a workday and you're tired and bored.

ii. **Routine:** Stand up, walk outside for fresh air for 15 minutes.

iii. **Reward:** Temporary escape from boredom, blood circulation and energy.

This is a small-game example simply to highlight the point of keeping the reward but changing the routine.

So how might you apply this in your life?

For example, perhaps you always say yes when someone needs your help. Your payoff is you get to feel good about helping someone (and avoiding feeling guilty for saying no). Yet this leads to a lifetime of never having time for yourself.

How can you discover a way to maintain the reward – avoiding guilt and experiencing worthiness of helping someone – yet changing the routine of saying yes every single time someone asks for help. (Hint: this is where your intentions will help you hone in on a creative solution.)

Abstain temporarily

In *Getting Unstuck: Break Free from the Plateau Effect*, the authors Hugh Thompson and Bob Sullivan challenge you to "kill your favorite thing," with the intent of bringing it back to life in a new way. I like this mindset when it comes to interrupting some of your favorite – or most pervasive – patterns.

For example, I've done:

- » no alcohol for 100 days
- » no TV/No Netflix for 90 days
- » no gluten, dairy, caffeine, dessert or gum for 30 days
- » no cell phone while on my couch or in my bedroom (I ended up keeping these indefinitely).

The intent is never to give up on these things entirely. Rather, to develop a relationship with them where I have a conscious choice – versus being in a perpetual state of drift.

Whenever I've abstained from something like the above, I always come out the other side with a command over these things that I couldn't access previously.

For example, Netflix became a compulsive habit for me. At the end of every night I found myself watching at least one or two hours. I decided to disrupt myself for 30 days. No TV, no Netflix. (I went on to do 50 days, and then another stretch of 90 days.)

> ***What I discovered was that Netflix was what I used as an escape – a way to shut out the never-ending chatter in my mind.***

There's nothing wrong with relaxing. Upon reflection, about an hour of Netflix would do the relaxation trick. But anything past an hour would put me in a state of restlessness, which led to a shorter night's sleep (and lower quality of sleep).

The feedback was: Netflix wasn't the enemy; it was the *amount* of Netflix. One episode of a show = good. Two or more episodes of a show = not good. Disrupting the pattern gave me this feedback, so I could adjust accordingly.

Some of my clients have tested:

- » no eating after 8:00pm for 30 days

- » no cell phone 20 minutes before sleep for 14 days

- » no cell phone within 20 minutes of awaking for 14 days

- » no glass of wine before bed for 30 days

- » no Facebook/Instagram for a weekend.

Start with abstaining from something for seven days. Get a win under your belt. Then you can graduate to longer periods (14, 21, or 30 days).

For bonus points, to make sure you stick to your guns, publicly announce your more challenging goals, like no alcohol for 100 days. When you declare your intentions to others, it's harder to not follow through. The stakes are too high.

Tell at least three friends when you take on a temporary abstinence challenge. They will keep you accountable, and your chances of success will double.

Remember, this abstinence is *temporary*. Commit to a specific time frame to pause a certain way of being. Set your intention in advance. Get clear on what you hope to learn or change as a result of this temporary abstinence, and also be open to receiving insights you didn't anticipate.

2. Declutter (reduce/remove)

A few decades ago we had a few dozen TV channels. Today we have a few thousand.

At one time, we may have had only five or six apps on our smartphone, and now we have fifty or sixty.

We live in an era of abundance, and it's not just limited to technology, information and material possessions. The era of abundance also extends to the choices, responsibilities, relationships and goals you allow into your life. And herein lies the problem:

You're letting too much stuff in.

While there may be a multi-billion dollar self-storage industry to hold onto your excess possessions, there's no such place to offload the intangible stuff you continue to take on.

This means you're accumulating a ridiculous amount of clutter in your life, and you're unconscious to its effect on you.

Clutter is a smokescreen used to avoid the most critical issues in your life.

Some of my clients clutter their lives by saying yes to way too many social opportunities that consume a shitload of their time but add very little in return. Others never feel like they're doing enough, so they start two businesses, sit on a charity board, coach their kid's soccer team, train for a marathon, do a juice cleanse and write a weekly blog on woodworking.

There's an insatiable movement to "get more done," and "be more productive." But when you're fighting infinite abundance, you're fighting a war you're set up to lose.

And you're showing up as a fraction of the powerful human being that you could be.

Prune your rosebush

I'm a big fan of Dr. Henry Cloud's writing. He's the author of several practical and thought-provoking personal development books.

In *Necessary Endings*, he offers up a useful analogy of "The Rosebush."

A rosebush by its very nature breeds more life than it physically can sustain. Without the care of an expert pruner, the rosebush will generate too many rosebuds and ultimately collapse in on itself and die.

Can you see the parallel in our own lives?

The sheer amount of "stuff" you're exposed to is extraordinary. You have access to more options, choices, information, and relationships in one week than your not-so-ancient ancestors had in an entire lifetime.

How do you sort it all?

Dr. Cloud offers three types of rosebuds to prune in order to "move forward."

i. The dead rosebuds

These are the easiest to identify. These are habits, relationships, activities and behaviors that simply don't serve you anymore and don't stand a chance of coming back to life. Snip!

ii. The atrophied rosebuds

These are tough. These are the buds that you say "well, if I just invest more time and energy, I can bring this (fill in the blank) back to life." And you may very well do so. But at what expense? For every ounce of energy invested into the atrophied rosebud, you deny that energy towards a potential great rosebud. Snip!

iii. The good rosebuds

These are the toughest of all. The argument here is that good rosebuds clog up the paths for great ones to grow. When you live in the era of abundance, you'll have no shortage of access to "good." Yet for you, "good" eventually becomes too easy. Too uninspiring. Too... *more of the same.* SNIP!

Marie Kondo's book *The Life-Changing Magic of Tidying Up* offers a simple but life-changing contrarian viewpoint on tidying up your rosebushes:

Instead of looking for what to throw out, only keep what gives you joy.

On September 5th 2016, I had a go at my wardrobe using her approach. I literally removed every article of clothing I owned and dumped it into a pile in my living room. The result?

Only one third of my wardrobe actually gave me joy. I ended up donating two thirds of my clothes.

If I'd taken the traditional approach, looking for what to get rid of, the ratios would've flipped. It was easy to identify a third of my clothes that I no longer needed. But some I rationalized keeping for a variety of reasons – sentimental value, it was a gift, I spent a lot of money on it. When I asked myself: "Does this bring me joy?" it was clear what stayed and what went. Amazingly, the whole process took me 90 minutes.

> *This experience helped me build a muscle that I brought into all contexts of my life: "Does this bring me joy?"*

Try it for yourself and see.

3. Experiment (add/test)

The third and final way to disrupt yourself is through running experiments. Experimentation is adding or testing something new that you haven't tried before, which can be a lot of fun (and sometimes scary).

No one runs more experiments than scientists, so let's take a page from their book to set us up for success:

» Scientists test hypotheses – suppositions that serve as the basis for further investigation. Instead of a hypothesis, you will be setting an intention. For example, "I'm going to read one book on leadership every month for three months to learn how to stop micromanaging my team."

» Scientists set timeframes for the length of their experiment. So will you.

» Scientists observe the results of their experiments dispassionately. They put aside being wrong or right. Rather, insights and feedback are gold, especially because those may turn out to be even more valuable than the original hypothesis. The same goes for your experiments.

Your experiments can be small, like the example of reading leadership books. Or you can concoct something more elaborate, like one of my most transformative experiments: A ten-day silent meditation.

A silent science experiment

You see, I have a hyperactive mind. It's always thinking, projecting, creating, worrying, fantasizing ... I can't ever seem to quiet it for any meaningful period of time (sound familiar?).

I wanted a way to disrupt my mind. So, like a scientist:

» **I set my intention**
To challenge my comfort zones, to sit with my mind without reacting and to generate new ways of responding to my thoughts and feelings.

» **I identified a specified period of time**
Ten days.

» **I observed dispassionately and collected feedback**
Sitting through ten days of silence, there ain't much to do anyway.

This was a scary proposition for me. But remember, one of my intentions was to challenge my comfort zone. So at the end of March 2016, I took a vow of silence for ten days. No talking, reading, writing, exercising, sexual activity...

just 11 hours a day of meditation and going inwards to connect with myself.

The first two days were intense. My mind was on hyperdrive. I was fantasizing and dreaming about being anywhere else just to escape the discomfort.

But on day three, something strange happened. My mind surrendered to my new reality. I was going to be here for another seven days, so I might as well adjust and accept the conditions. For the remainder of the retreat, I entered a state of calm, creativity and awareness that I'd never experienced before.

A year later, that experiment continues to pay dividends in my ability to listen to (but not react to) my mind, to quickly overcome challenging situations, to elevate my pain threshold (both physically and emotionally) and access a heightened level of patience and compassion for other people.

Not a bad ROI for a single experiment.

FREE YOURSELF FIRST

One of my clients, Paul, is a highly successful financial advisor with a multi-billion dollar book of business, and a single father of two beautiful boys. He's in his mid-40s and had never taken a vacation without taking his work with him.

One of the reasons Paul got into the advisor business, ironically, was freedom. Freedom to steer his ship as he saw fit. Yet *for decades*, Paul had never experienced a true break from work. How much freedom is there in that?

As much as he loved his business, the never-ending grind was becoming exhausting. As the rainmaker and number one guy for his clients, he never even questioned the story, "I have to be available to my clients."

So I challenged his limiting story.

First, I brought his awareness to the fact his freedom, which was a core value of his, was stifled. And then I showed him the possibility of having an unplugged vacation through sharing my own successes in making that transition. The combination of these two led to his awakening – a willingness to make a change and take action.

The next step was for Paul to disrupt his typical vacation pattern (of staying plugged in).

Paul had a dream of renting a Ducati and riding solo up the Pacific Coast Highway. No plan, no interruptions, just him and the road. Perfect.

For that experience to become reality, he had to disrupt his normal pattern of "business as usual," which meant not bringing his laptop and work cell on this trip. He also had to prepare his clients that he would be unreachable for five days. Here's the note he sent his clients:

> *I wanted to let you both know I will be taking a few days of vacation next week. A real one!*
>
> *I will be in California, and on Tuesday I will be hopping on a motorcycle and riding the Pacific Coast Highway for five days.*

*I will return to work on Tuesday, September 20th. If not,
I may be a bartender in an obscure California town.*

*I have no destination planned, just a general direction.
I am armed with a go-pro, my camera, an American
Express card and few dead presidents.*

*If you need anything you already know you are
in good hands.*

*Sharon will be taking care of any issues. She will
coordinate any individuals from the service team,
Daniel, Jennifer, and/or Julie if needed.*

*By the way, don't email me. I will be deleting the email
from my iPhone on Tuesday at 10:00am PST!*

Adventure waits,

Paul

If this sounds bold, it's only because you haven't tried it before. Paul's clients *loved it*. They cheered him on and praised him for setting off on a "not to be bothered" adventure.

When Paul came back, he was stunned to learn that he'd received about 25% of the typical email and calls he'd been used to. He called me in a semi-panic wondering if this was a sign of a problem.

"Hell no," I said. "It's a sign that you nailed the communication process before you left. Mission success."

Once Paul had successfully disrupted his former pattern, he had an even deeper sense of awakening around the true power he held to take command of his future.

Clarity breeds energy

My mentor Strategic Coach Lee Brower (who was featured in the bestselling book *The Secret*) always says "clarity breeds energy." In other words, if you are clear on your mission, you naturally summon the energy to change and charge forward.

You can instantly tell when someone is unclear on where they are heading in life. At one extreme, there are those who act with a harried freneticism in everything they do. Their energy is scattered and directionless. Everything is urgent and they are constantly stressed out. At the other extreme, there is an absence of energy ... a lifelessness. There is such a lack of clarity that there's no need for energy production.

You MUST get clear on the future you *can't wait to live into*. Disrupting your existing way of living is designed to facilitate that clarity.

Remember, 95% of your thoughts, feelings and behaviors are automatic, unconscious and habitual. When you allow that 95% to put you on extended autopilot, you've found yourself in a state of drift (the Devil's playground).

Disrupting allows you to break free from Drift on your own terms.

It also is an instigator for the following three things:

1. Accelerated feedback

When you disrupt a pattern, you accelerate feedback about why that habit exists, what feelings you experience in the absence of the habit, and how that habit is serving or hijacking your life.

If you're on the wrong path, you want to know immediately because you can always adjust. And if you're on the right path, you can accelerate even faster. But the key here is accelerating your exposure to feedback so you can stay in motion.

2. Deeper awakenings

Remember, an awakening is that tipping point where you are ready to take action. Once you are in action around disruption, you'll generate feedback, which inevitably leads to deeper awakenings.

For example, one of my clients wanted to improve his "comfort eating" habits. He would come home from work, overload his plate and gorge himself. He wouldn't stop when he was full. As Louis CK would say, he wouldn't stop eating until "he hated himself."

So he·and I did a hypnosis session where we simulated him coming home from work and heading towards his meal. We stopped him right before taking that first bite, and I prompted him to tune into his feelings. What he found was a powerful feeling that he interpreted as "if I don't eat, I might die."

Upon further inspection, this was a story rooted in his younger years, where food was very much tied to his survival (on a number of personal levels.) While this feeling was antiquated and not at all useful given his current lifestyle, it was still operating as strong as ever, playing out in his unconscious behaviors.

This disruption (via hypnosis and breaking down his eating process) gave him an even deeper awakening that provided a further catalyst for change.

3. "Design" ideas

Accelerated feedback and deeper awakenings facilitate a clarity that previously eluded you. This clarity allows to better envision the future you want to live into, which catalyzes your ability to start designing that future right now (which we will look at in depth in the next chapter).

I've always had a lot of fun disrupting my own bad habits because it leads to tremendous personal growth. And it's exhilarating when I can do the same for my clients because [XYZ]. Find ways for yourself to make it light, creative and fun so you can keep designing a future you can't wait to live into.

CHAPTER 4

DESIGNING

"I'm so excited that I can barely sit still or hold a thought in my head. I think it's the excitement only a free man can feel. A free man at the start of a long journey whose conclusion is uncertain."

- RED, SHAWSHANK REDEMPTION

This is one of the greatest quotes from one of the greatest movies of all time (don't try to argue with me on that one...)

Red, played by Morgan Freeman, finds himself a free man after four decades of imprisonment for a questionable crime he committed as a teenager. For the first time in his adult life, he's unshackled. He can go anywhere and do anything. He can design his future ... as a free man.

At this stage, you might feel a lot like Red. While his prison bars were real and physical; you've been quarantined by the invisible shackles of your unconscious beliefs, stories and patterns. Just like Red, your freedom has been inhibited.[13]

Having had an awakening, however, you became conscious to these things. Through the process of disrupting, you've bent those bars and are ready to step outside the walls that have contained you for so long.

Now you, like Red, are "a free man (or woman) at the start of a long journey whose conclusion is uncertain."

---

13 Except he knew it, and you didn't.

If that doesn't light you up, then check your pulse!

At this stage of the ADD Cycle, you've generated enough insights and feedback to have a compelling sense of what type of future you want to live into, so now it's time to start designing that future.

Designing a future you can't wait to live into involves three steps:

1. **Believe** you have *ultimate authority* over your life.

2. **Write** your own eulogy.

3. **Take command** of your next 90 days.

Remember, the ADD Cycle is called a "cycle" for a reason. Designing isn't a set-and-forget activity. Whatever you design is going to create new awakenings in your life, causing you to disrupt your patterns again, which will lead to a new design. Go into this process with the intention to design, execute, and then repeat the cycle of awakening again.

Let's begin.

STEP 1: BELIEVE YOU HAVE ULTIMATE AUTHORITY OVER YOUR LIFE

Remember Figure 1.1: Beliefs, stories and behaviors?

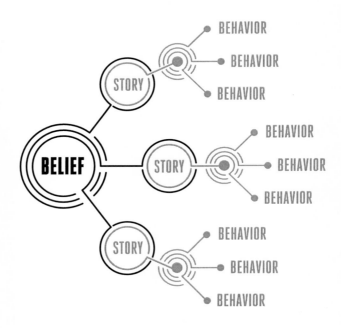

Beliefs are what you hold to be true at the deepest level of your being. A knowing that goes beyond words or conscious detection. They are the seeds that spawn the stories you tell about yourself and the world around you. Those stories sprout your behaviors.

A single belief is responsible for an unlimited number of negative, but also positive, behaviors in your life. Beliefs are choices. So you can choose to install an empowering belief, and the entire world around you transforms.

Designing a future you can't wait to live into requires you to consciously choose this belief:

You have ultimate authority over your life.

Ultimate authority means taking responsibility for the fact that your life is the sum total of every decision you've ever made from the day you were born up until this very moment. This means you get to take credit for the many successes you've had. It also means the shit parts of your life are on you too.

Ultimate authority means if you're working 70 hours a week, trapped in a career you have no passion for and stuck in a sexless marriage, then you assume full responsibility for it. Your choices led you here. Your choices will also lead you to higher ground.

Like Stephen Pressfield says in his must-read book *The War of Art*, "We have two lives. The life we live, and the unlived life within us."

Ultimate authority allows you to access that unlived life within you.

Ultimate authority is the knowing that you have infinite power to create the world around you.

Believing in ultimate authority is hard. It isn't for everyone.

It means feeling the pain that comes with owning your shit. Accepting responsibility for one's own life condition is too massive and terrifying for most.

Non-believers are victims of external circumstance. They avoid pain by shirking responsibility for the condition of their life. Their strategy for change is based on hope, not action.

Non-believers blame.

Non-believers wait.

Non-believers drift.

Drifting is the devil's territory.

It's easy to identify those who have claimed their ultimate authority:

- » They're the ones riding the biggest waves.

- » They're the ones who everyone else is talking about.

- » They're the ones leading the charge.

- » They're the ones who make the decisions others won't.

- » They're the ones having the most fun.

So how do you reclaim your *ultimate authority*?

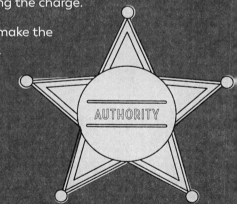

Put your money where you're mouth is

Ultimate authority is an empty term until you step up to the plate and put your money where your mouth is. Here's a tangible example of how to reclaim your ultimate authority in a real-life situation.

» **Make an inventory**

Take a moment now to do a quick inventory of the parts of your life where you feel most powerless. Maybe it's your relentless schedule, your deteriorating relationship, your financial situation or whatever is holding you back.

» **Say goodbye**

Then take whatever excuse you've been using up to this point – for example, "Our sex life stopped after our son was

born" – and have a funeral for it. You can't use it anymore. Your power to change your situation lies exclusively within you.

» **Own it**

Now own the situation at hand by telling the truth about why and how you ended up here. It may sound something like, "I've been complaining about how busy my life is. I've blamed it on the demands of my job and having three young children. The truth is, I take on way too many responsibilities at work, because if I say no I feel like my colleagues will think I'm soft. So I overextend myself, I come home exhausted and I half ass my time with my kids before I pass out on the couch. From this point forward, I will not blame my life condition on my job or my children. I chose to say yes to those job commitments and I chose to have a family. Therefore I take full responsibility for the life I've created."

» **Declare**

When you own your situation, you reclaim your ultimate authority. Now you have full power to transform your situation. Declare your new intentions and state the actions you will take to create your new future. For example, "I will wind down my involvement on two work projects that consume hours of my time because I'm not essential to their completion. I'll communicate to the project leader within the next 48 hours and transition my work before week's end. I will use that extra time to get home early and see my children with my best energy."

Follow these steps, and you'll be amazed at how quickly your ultimate authority rises to the occasion.

STEP 2: WRITE YOUR OWN EULOGY

Whenever I present the "you're going to be writing your own eulogy" step to my clients, I usually get a response ranging from discomfort to downright resistance.

Well, good. That means I'm onto something. (In parts of Asia, especially Japan, there are even particular festivals that let you take a test run of your funeral with coffins, clothes, makeup, blankets, and more.)

In the past, I've attempted to stretch people's thinking by asking them to define their purpose in life. By in large, this approach fails. People don't know where to begin, so they end up stabbing around for the typical platitudes of "I want to be a devoted husband/wife" and "dedicated father/mother," and "someone who has given way more than he/she has asked for."

Or, it becomes a laundry list of career accolades and achievements.

Not that any of these things aren't great. But they're usually generated by what people *think* they should say, versus something that actually *inspires* them.

As David Brooks, author of *The Moral Bucket List*, once said:

> Our culture and our educational systems spend more time teaching the skills and strategies you need for career success than the qualities you need to radiate that sort of inner light. Many of us are clearer on how to build an external career than on how to build inner character.

Society places so much emphasis on building and celebrating what Brooks calls resume virtues, those skills you bring to the marketplace, that there is very little guidance out there on how to build the eulogy virtues, the ones talked about at your funeral, like whether you were kind, honest or brave.

We need a more empowering context to shift the conversation.

Something happens when you are forced to confront the reality of your own death. This truth forces you to evaluate the setup of your life today, and whether it supports the person you want to be when you leave this planet.

It also creates clarity and necessary urgency to perform the actions now and into the immediate future that will shape your legacy.

Clarity regarding "the end" drives clarity "now"

So where do you begin?

A eulogy can be as long as you like or as short as you like, but it has to have enough substance and meaning that will catalyze a change. You don't need to be a professional writer to be able to write a eulogy. But I appreciate that you might feel uncomfortable with the experience at first and have no idea where to begin.

So to start, jot down answers to the following four questions:

1. How long do you want to live?

Notice I didn't say, "How long do you *think* you'll live?" This distinction is critically important. Don't get caught up in family history, genetics and actual probabilities.

One of my clients always believed he would die in his early 60s. Why? Because his father died in his 60s, as did his grandfather. He simply accepted that would be his fate too. Do you think that belief affected how he treated himself? Damn right it did. He always had trouble regulating a healthy diet. His weight yo-yoed, he would overdrink and over party. But it didn't matter because he believed he'd be dying young anyway.

When he went through this exercise, it illuminated how silly that unchecked belief was. On his very first stab at it, he added an extra ten years to his lifespan (I'm continuing to push him for more), and it immediately catalyzed his efforts to get healthier now. After all, if he's going to live an extra ten years, he better start acting like it, right?

So how long do

RUN FREE

In 2011, Faujah Singh became the first 100-year-old person in the history of the world to complete a marathon, finishing the Toronto Waterfront Marathon in eight hours, 11 minutes and six seconds.

He did it again at the age of 101, finishing the London Marathon in seven hours and 49 minutes. He carried the torch at the 2012 London Olympics.

He didn't even take up running until the age of 81, after his wife had passed. And he wasn't able to walk until the age of five because of a birth defect.

At the writing of this book, Singh is 104 years old and is still running strong.

2. How boldly can you envision your future?

You may be so deeply rooted in the constraints of today that you're at risk of shortchanging the unlimited potential waiting to be unlocked in the years and decades ahead of you. Flipping this mindset is crucial.

Here are some examples of "current realities" that you can let go of:

» You're the breadwinner in the family therefore you must maintain a safe job with steady income.

» You have four children and outside of work they get 99.9% of your attention.

» You've never been an entrepreneur, but the idea fascinates and terrifies you.

» Current life expectancy for adults in America is 78.74 years.

It's so easy to get caught up in the way things are right now, and feel like it's going to continue this way forever. But that's not the case at all. Especially not when you're playing the long game, i.e. *the rest of your life*. You've got decades left of living to do. Anything can happen. When you've got a blank canvas and a palette, you can paint anything. There are no constraints.

Right now the average life expectancy for a US citizen is 78.74 years. But that number is going up every year, and with some of the technological advancements coming, scientists are projecting dramatic shifts in longevity. In fact, compelling research has shown evidence that the first person to live to 150 is already walking this planet. Crazy right? Only if you constrain yourself to the reality of our times. For every new baby born, 150 is very much a reality of their existence.

It's incredibly useful to take such things into consideration when writing your eulogy. I did. My first eulogy had me living until 120.[14] Because I have eight decades left to live, it inspires me to invest in my

14 One of my clients informed me that 121 would take me to the year 2100, so of course now I'm living to 121!

wellbeing physically, mentally, emotionally, spiritually every single day. With that much time on my side, it's easy to dream big. With that much potential to create anything, I act now.

The same goes for you. Just because you have three children under the age of five, a seven-figure mortgage and a woefully under-funded 529 plan doesn't mean those conditions will exist the rest of your life. Use this opportunity to dream up your ideal. How you get there is unimportant at this stage; finding what's inspiring is.

3. Who do you want to be in all the days ahead?

Dream up any version of yourself that you choose. Envision who you want to be for all the years left ahead of you, and write about that person.

I once failed to give this guidance to a client of mine. The eulogy he'd written was touching, inspiring and beautiful. But 95% of it would be true if he were to have died on the day he read it to me (even though he projected he'd live another four decades.) This is your opportunity to THINK BIG.

You'd be surprised by how many people believe their glory days are behind them. Hell, even The Boss sang one of the greatest songs of all time about this.

Believing your best days are behind you is toxic. Yet so many people unwittingly adopt this belief. Which feeds their stories. Which fuels their behaviors.

Someone once said: "Isn't it a wonderful thought, to know that our best days are yet to come?"

If that were true for you, what unforgettable experiences did you have? What did you accomplish? What relationships did you forge?

4. What legacy do you want to leave behind?

What lives on beyond you? What dent did you put into the universe that can't be undone because of you? What contributions did you make?

You get extra smiles if you include how your work contributed to your legacy. I've recently added this one to my guidelines because most of my clients will say to me. "Work didn't show up anywhere in my eulogy. It shows how unimportant work is in the grand scheme of life!"

Whoa, not so fast. Work is essential to building a meaningful legacy. Your work provides the income and foundation to support the most important things in your life. Even if you're currently disconnected from the work you're doing, the eulogy exercise is a tremendous way to illuminate how you can align your future self with how you show up at work presently.

For example, my eulogy remembers me for how creative and forward thinking I was. But at the time I'd written it, I was bringing only a fraction of my creative potential to my job. So I decided to start right then and there. I became bolder in the ideas I brought to the workplace. I challenged convention. Soon, I got a spark back for the work I'd been doing that had been missing for a while.

DOMINICK'S EULOGY

(Written March 13th, 2017)

Eulogy dated: January 7th, 2100

The day before Dominick Quartuccio's passing at the age of 121, he was doing what he loved: speaking to friends, family and devoted followers about creating the futures of their dreams.

Born November 7th, 1978, to father Dominick Sr., mother Amy and sister Mary. He was a loving son, brother, father, grandfather, and great grandfather.

Dominick left a legacy of love for people. He had an insatiable interest in other people, seeing people how they wanted to be seen. The highest compliment he ever received was, "You make me love myself when I'm in your presence." It was a compliment he received often.

His life's purpose was to constantly strive to be the best version of himself and help other people do the same. The people whose lives he touched became better husbands, wives, parents, children, business owners, workers, and humans. The communities they impacted created a ripple effect felt across the world.

During his lifetime, he spoke to and trained over one million people. Dominick was the author of a dozen books, selling millions of copies worldwide, including five New York Times bestsellers.

Dominick was an avid adventurer. He visited over 100 countries and made five trips to outer space. He was always experimenting on his mind, body, and soul in his unrelenting drive for continuous growth.

He remained active and healthy throughout his life, exercising regularly up until the year before his passing.

For the last 20 years of his life, Dominick hosted an annual weeklong retreat for his entire family in a surprise destination. He called it "The Ultimate Tribe." His family fondly refers to it as "the most exciting week" of their lives every year. His son, Dominick III will now assume the responsibilities and carry on this tradition.

Dominick is survived by his three children, seven grandchildren and 11 great-grandchildren.

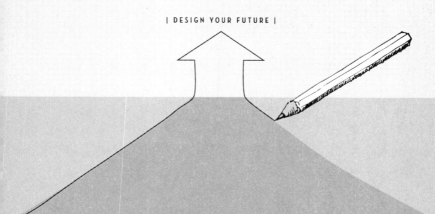

STEP 3: TAKE COMMAND OF YOUR NEXT 90 DAYS

The idea of living your legacy on a day-to-day, hour-to-hour minute-to-minute basis isn't practical. You need to chunk it down to a near-term vision, create a constraint that provides urgency, and implement a rock-solid plan for execution.

You need to learn to *take command of your next 90 days.*

Most people fail in their pursuit of larger goals because either they are too overwhelmed with the magnitude of it (where do I begin?) or they're operating in an undefined period of time without deadlines so they don't move with proper urgency. A 90-day focus solves both problems.

This is long enough to achieve extraordinary results, and yet short enough for you to feel the urgency of every day.

To construct a 90-day plan of attack follow these guidelines.

Establish compelling goals

By the end of your 90 days, you want a tangible result. The thing that you want may take three years to achieve, but you can put a hefty dent in it in the next 90 days. So here's where you breakdown the complex and start chopping down the redwood.

These are your criteria for establishing compelling goals:

» **They must be something that inspires you**
You are designing a future you can't wait to live into. Picking goals based on what you think you "should" do or what others expect of you won't cut it.

» **They must be slightly out of reach**
Optimally designed goals have a hint of "shit, can I really do that?" firmly embedded in them. Raising the bar requires you to raise your game. Knocking down goals like these is deeply rewarding, and facilitates you leveling up the next time.

» **They must be tied to your legacy (eulogy) virtues**
Designing goals any other way would be like
driving east when your GPS says west. From this
point forward, everything you design is consciously
aligned with the legacy you're building.

Here are some examples of goals that my clients
have chosen:

» Lose 20 pounds and 5% body fat.

» Declutter my office by digitally scanning
every document and going paperless.

» Increase the sales team's pipeline to $3.5B.

» Plan and take one adventure (minimum five
days) while completely disconnected from work.

» Unwind 100% of my interests
in a fledgling business.

Here's one piece of guidance you cannot ignore, especially
as you're starting this for the first time:

Pick ONE major goal, and that's it.

I mean it! Your life is already over-committed. You simply won't have the bandwidth to tackle three new goals while keeping all your other balls in the air.

My high-achieving clients always ignore this advice. They get so excited about taking on two or three major goals – because after all, they're achievers! – only to find they lose steam 30 to 40 days in. This is natural, and I'll talk more about it in the next chapter. The key factor at play here is that the energy required to start something is entirely different than the energy required to sustain something.[15] That's why you may find yourself failing to follow through on commitments you've made. Then you get pissed at yourself and it's a big damn mess. Let's just avoid that altogether, shall we?

---

15 If you've ever been in a relationship, you know exactly what I'm talking about.

Especially as you're getting started, it's best to stick with one major goal and see it through.

The One Thing: The Surprisingly Simple Truth Behind Extraordinary Results by Gary Keller is a phenomenal book that hammers home this point far better than I ever could. I highly recommend giving it a read.

Get clear on the desired results

Hitting a goal is like crossing the finish line of a race. But what about everything that happens after hitting the finish line? Why did you run the race to begin with?

That's where this step comes in.

Let's say your 90-day goal is to lose 20 pounds and reduce your body fat by 5%. Why is this important? If you tell me it's because you'll feel better about yourself and fit into your clothes, that's just weak. The juice isn't worth the squeeze, and you'll give up.

If you tell me, however, something like:

» My partner can't keep their hands off of me. Our sex is the best it's been in years.

» I have gotten my mojo back. I walk with confidence into every room I enter.

» I've reduced the likelihood that I will need to go on medication that will dull my senses and cause me to show up as a fraction of myself.

NOW you're talking. These are the types of juicy outcomes that will keep you going long after the initial motivation wears off.

So ask yourself: What is the result you desire after 90 days of each goal? Then write it down.

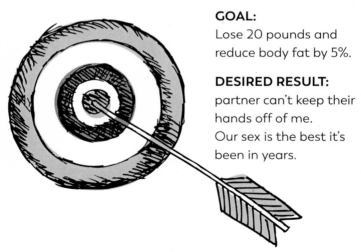

GOAL:
Lose 20 pounds and reduce body fat by 5%.

DESIRED RESULT:
partner can't keep their hands off of me.
Our sex is the best it's been in years.

Goal:
_____
_____

Desired result:
_____
_____

Goal:
_____
_____

Desired result:
_____
_____

Goal:
_____
_____

Desired result:
_____
_____

Outline the actions

You won't always have control over whether you can achieve your goal. However, you have total control over your actions.

You need to get clear on the big actions that you have control over that must be completed by the end of the 90 days in order to hit your goal. Then you need to chunk those 90-day actions down to smaller, achievable weekly actions.

Salespeople know the drill on this one. While I was at Prudential, my salespeople were assigned a goal of bringing in $200,000,000 in new investment assets every year. They couldn't control which companies were looking to move business in that calendar year. What they could control, however, were how many phone calls they'd make to generate the type of activity that could lead to that $200,000,000.

Going back to the losing 20 pounds example, 90-day actions might look like this:

- » Over the next 90 days I will work out 50 times for 30 to 60 minutes apiece.

» I will not eat after 8:00pm on weekdays.

» I will have successfully implemented
a sustainable nutritional program
to maintain my new weight.

Those are big actions. So the Week One actions might look like this:

» Schedule workouts for Monday,
Wednesday, Friday and Saturday.

» On Wednesday I have a business
dinner at 8:00pm, so I'll schedule
Saturday as a makeup day.

» Ask friends for three recommendations
on nutritionists, and schedule exploratory
calls with them before the week is over.

If you choose the appropriate actions and execute on them, chances are you'll hit or exceed your goal.

You might like to use the Vision Executor, Figure 4.1, to help you fill out and track your 90-day goals, actions and impacts.

	GOAL ONE	GOAL TWO
90 DAY GOAL (Your goal in one sentence)		
DESIRED RESULTS AND IMPACT (What must be true if goal is achieved)		
ACTIONS THAT MUST BE COMPLETED BY END OF 90 DAYS (Lead indicators)		
WEEK 1 ACTION PLAN (Actions that must be completed by end of week)		

Figure 4.1: Vision Executor

Download and use the Vision Executor to help you fill out your 90-day goals, actions and impacts: dominickq.com/resources

Create a scorecard

It's critical to track your progress against the actions you committed to. Creating a simple scorecard is the best way to do this. It not only helps focus your attention, but you will also experience a sense of accomplishment each time you get to put a check mark in the box.

For example, for one 30-day period in my 90-day focus I decided to do no TV/Netflix, no desserts, and get eight hours of sleep per night. On an index card, I created a mini calendar and each time I carried through on my action, I put a check next to it. When I didn't I left it blank. Simple as that.

Over those 30 days, I got to see all those checkmarks pile up, increasing my confidence in my ability to execute on my goals.

Figure 4.2 is an example of a simple scorecard you can create to track your progress.

DATE	MEDITATE FOR 15 MINS	SLEEP FOR 7 – 8 HOURS	NO ALCOHOL
Wednesday, March 1	x	x	x
Thursday, March 2	x		x
Friday, March 3	x	x	x
Saturday, March 4,	x	x	
Sunday, March 5,	x	x	x
Monday, March 6	x	x	x
Tuesday, March 7	x		x
Wednesday, March 8	x	x	
Thursday, March 9	x	x	x
Friday, March 10	x	x	x

Figure 4.2: A simple scorecard

THE CHEESESTEAK STRUCTURE (YES, REALLY)

I lived in Philly for two years. During that time, I ate my bodyweight in cheesesteaks (a few times over).

Everyone knows what makes a cheesesteak great: the roll. Sure, the meat in between matters. But if you get a soggy, shitty roll ... or a hard stale roll ... it doesn't matter what comes in between.

The same principle applies to how you structure your days. Your evening and morning rituals are the bookends to your day. Those rituals determine the quality of what happens throughout the day.

So the question becomes, what exactly are your morning and evening rituals? And are they setting you up to hit your goals or not?

Here's a simple exercise to practice for the next seven days:

1. Take inventory of the last hour of your day.

2. Take inventory of the first hour of your day.

3. Record everything that you do sequentially.

For example, your morning may look something like:

- 6:00am = wakeup

- 6:00 – 6:15am = review texts and emails that came in while you were sleeping

- 6:15 – 6:45am = shower, get dressed, while listening to CNN/Fox news

- 6:45 – 7:00am = scroll Facebook, LinkedIn and Instagram feeds

No matter how small the detail, record it. Wherever your attention is directed, whatever behavior you demonstrate, whatever you do ... record it for seven days. (Don't forget to record your evening ritual.)

You'll be amazed by how many little rituals you've implemented that are standing in the way of hitting your goals.

Once you've finished the observation process, start to implement rituals that ensure your success. For example, if you want to establish a morning workout routine, a supporting ritual would look like:

"If I have a workout scheduled for the next day, I will lay out my sneakers and gym clothes the night before in a visible place."

Eventually the ritual, which starts with a conscious choice and some discipline upfront, will turn into an unconscious habit (the 95% is on your side!)

NO MORE DRIFTING

When I was in my early 30s, I'd have these nights where I'd be so anxious about my future that I couldn't fall asleep. Even if I was exhausted, I'd be completely wired and there'd be a painful wrenching in my gut. Something was telling me that I wasn't in command of my life.

These anxiety attacks only happened every six months or so, but they were powerful enough to send a charge of fear that struck me to my core.

During that time of my life, I was drifting. My life was happening to me. Those nights of restlessness were forcing me to face the reality that the rest of my life would be one big question mark if I continued to sit in the passenger seat of my own life.

I haven't had one of those nights in at least five years. That's because now, I'm actively designing my future using the blueprint I shared with you in this chapter.

It's not always easy. But I'm in command of my future, and that's profound.

I'll end this chapter where I started it, with Red, and one revision:

> *"I'm so excited that I can barely sit still or hold a thought in my head. I think it's the excitement only a free man can feel. A free man at the start of a long journey —into a future he can't wait to live into."*

FUTURE

The cycle never ends.
It's up to you now.

CHAPTER 5

SUSTAINING

---

*"History will be kind to me
for I intend to write it."*

- WINSTON CHURCHILL

I was speaking at an event recently for Foreign Policy Interrupted, a movement designed to elevate women in media's voices in international news. The audience was full of writers and aspiring authors. In fact, most had dreamed of writing a book, and many of them had started, but very few had finished.

So I held up a book, *From the Other Side of the World*, authored by one of the founders of Foreign Policy Interrupted, Elmira Bayrasli.

I said "Elmira, are there mistakes in this book?"

"Yes, there are," she said.

"Are there things you wish you could go back and change?"

"Definitely."

"Do you kick yourself for forgetting to add a particular detail or story?"

"All the time."

Then I turned to the audience and said, "Yeah, but she's got a fucking book."

Your ability to sustain – and ultimately complete – the plan you've designed is the dividing line between a future of more of the same and a future you can't wait to live into.

Executing on a 90-day plan isn't easy. You will be fraught with resistance, distractions, perfectionism,[16] old habits and a litany of other obstacles to prevent you from finishing what you've started. It's easy to go off course, and even easier to stay there.

---

16 Like the authors who never finish writing their book.

In my experience, 80% of people who start a 90-day plan won't sustain it beyond the early stages; 5% of people will successfully execute from start to finish; and only 1% will execute over and over again.

I believe with the proper tools and planning, we can blow those numbers out of the water.

My intent is to equip you with the tools to avoid the most common pitfalls that sabotage your ability to finish what you started.

YOUR SUPER SEVEN SUSTAINING TIPS

There are seven things you need to keep in mind to sustain and complete your 90-day plan:

1. Be aware that it's way more exciting to start than to keep going

2. Avoid the "I suck at finishing things" story

3. Prepare for the energy downshift

4. Align everything with your legacy vision

5. Understand that perfectionism is the enemy of completion

6. Remember that something is better than nothing

7. Accumulate small wins

Let's cover each in more detail.

1. It's way more exciting to start than to keep going

Whether it's diving into *Atlas Shrugged*, starting the Whole 30 diet or attacking P90X, they all seem like amazing ideas until the honeymoon period ends

Even with the best of intentions, we abandon books after the first two chapters, go back on the cheesecake-only diet after a week of clean eating and give Tony Horton the heave-ho when the workouts become inconvenient.

The start of writing this book was *thrilling*. The concept came to me in a flash of inspiration. The first 5,000 words flowed from my fingers. I got to tell everyone I was writing a book and was showered with praise for it.

But when the reality set in that I had another 25,000 to 30,000 words to go ... and I had to edit it ... smooth out my rough transitions ... do research and make citations ... get the book typeset and published ... a lot of the shine rubbed off from the once sexy project.

It's exciting to start new shit.

It's not as exciting to finish shit.

I've got no empirical evidence to support this, but I believe nature rewards us when we start something new. Our body is flooded with that addictive euphoric chemical cocktail – with the likes of dopamine and endorphins – to get us into motion. Perhaps this is our evolutionary reward, because our advancement depends on it.

But our stingy brains and bodies only produce so much of the fun juice. Then it's on us to tap our additional resources (as you'll read about in the next few insights) to keep going.

2. Avoid the "I suck at finishing things" story

Because you've already got a bunch of unfinished projects or abandoned your fair share of others, it's tempting to create a story around your inability to see things through. You get gun shy in taking on new goals or you live out the self-fulfilling prophecy of "here I go again!"

Remember, your stories give birth to your behaviors, so first and foremost it's essential you create stories that generate the behaviors you want. If you're currently carrying the "I suck at finishing things" bag, put it down.

The new story becomes "I'm learning how to sustain and complete the things I take on." You become the learner. A learner is on the lookout for new techniques they hadn't sought out previously. They learn. They improve. They complete.

One more thing.

You wouldn't suck at building houses if I withheld nails and measuring tape from you. You'd be without the essential tools to complete the project. If you've struggled with finishing things in the past, it's likely because you didn't have a set of tools to help you navigate the journey from start to completion.

Now you have the nails and measuring tape that you've been missing. So there is really no excuse.

3. Prepare for the energy downshift

My one-on-one clients are the greatest. They're ultra-achieving world-beaters. When we start our 90-day coaching program, they outline massive and inspiring goals that would break the backs of a small army.

They're so excited and cocksure (I never miss an opportunity to drop that word) about their ability to slay the dragon that none of them heed my advice:

Be ready for the energy shift. It's coming.

After a polite acknowledgement, they brush it off and shoot out of the gates like thoroughbreds. On days seven, 14 and 21, they present their laundry lists of remarkable achievements with an attitude of invincibility.

Then, the energy shifts.

Usually around day 30 I'll get a phone call that's some version of, "Yeah I couldn't get to XYZ because last week was crazy, but I'll get back on track this week."

Then the next week, it'll be, "Man things have been crazy and I just haven't had the time to get to XYZ."

This is code for: The initial "high" has worn off, it's no longer sexy, other shit has popped up, and you're not feeling the same reward to keep going.

Here's my advice: Anticipate and embrace the downshift in energy. It means you've successfully moved through the first phase of implementation and now it's time to recalibrate for phase two.

This is why it's so important to align your design elements to your eulogy/legacy vision for yourself. When the initial high dissipates, reconnecting with the meaning and purpose of your actions will be essential to keep you going.

For example, my legacy vision includes "helping others achieve the highest version of themselves." Recently I was planning my first men's retreat, and found myself overwhelmed with the tasks of marketing, designing, following up, and troubleshooting all the details of the retreat. To top it all off, the interest was seemingly nonexistent in the early stages.

After the initial excitement of organizing a retreat wore off, this overwhelmed feeling and lack of interest easily could've allowed me to rationalize throwing in the towel. Instead, because this retreat was one step towards my legacy vision, I persisted.

A few weeks later, we sold out the retreat, transforming the lives of two-dozen men—and the communities they impact—in the process.

That wouldn't have been possible if I hadn't learned how to embrace the energy downshift.

4. Align everything with your legacy vision

What's the difference between eggs and ham?

The chicken is involved, but the pig is committed.

When it comes to the goals you've outlined, are you merely interested in them, or are you committed?

On occasion, my clients fall into this trap. Sometimes they'll target a flashy goal, like learning how to speed read or conquer Italian (both of which are cool). But when you have to continue dedicating precious hours to these endeavors, "cool" is not reason enough to sustain that kind of long-term activity.

At the other end of the spectrum there are goals with a perfectly rational argument for achieving them, like tackling another industry designation or joining a board of directors. Again, once the initial burst of energy wears off, these endeavors turn into obligations that become burdensome.

That's why the eulogy exercise is so important. You get clear on your legacy vision, which helps you to make more meaningful decisions in the moment.

I can't tell you how many times this insight helped me as I transitioned from a lucrative and comfortable corporate leadership role to a zero-client and zero-revenue entrepreneurial venture.

When I launched my blog in February of 2014, my first few installments generated massive buzz among my network. Viewership was strong and engagement was high. But a month later, as the novelty wore off, viewership and engagement dwindled to about 20% of those first few weeks.

The next three to six months were painful for me. I poured my heart and soul into every weekly blog post, only to hear crickets on more than a few occasions. If continuing my blog wasn't directly aligned with my legacy vision, I'd have abandoned it right then during that rough patch. Instead, I kept going.

Today, I have thousands of weekly readers. They share stories with me about how my insights have changed their lives. The visibility of my blog consistently generates coaching, speaking and training opportunities, which are the lifeblood of my business.

Over the course of my career, my ability to sustain this project will be worth millions. I remain committed because it aligns with my legacy vision.

5. Perfectionism is the enemy of completion

Back in 2010, Facebook's headquarters had this painted in big bold letters on its wall:

"Done is better than perfect."

Ultimately, perfectionism is a guise for fear. Fear of being judged or being attacked or having your flaws exposed or whatever other weird hang-up you're carrying.

The book you're reading is littered with so much imperfection it makes me cringe. But guess what? *I've got a book.* (Just like Elmira at the start of this chapter.)

This book gives me authority; it raises my speaking fees and gives me the prestigious title of "author." It allows me to make an impact in your life in a way that a short blog post or two-minute video can't. If I had allowed my perfectionism to take over, none of these benefits would have manifested.

Another angle to avoid perfectionism is to complete something—knowing it will be imperfect—and then use that opportunity to generate feedback, iterate and improve.

Technology companies do this all the time with what's called a Minimum Viable Product (MVP).

For example, when Uber first released their Minimum Viable Product, it didn't have a fraction of the cool features (shared rides, sending your GPS tracker to your friends etc.) that it has today. All they wanted to test was whether the heart of their technology worked: could you, the customer, connect with a driver to pick you up and would the automatic payment work?

At that point, they got the most critical thing: feedback.

Feedback quickly allows you to assess what's working, what isn't and where you can make tweaks to pivot. If you can step into the "MVP" mindset, the pressure for perfection dissipates.

Embrace imperfection on your way to completion, and you'll conquer the biggest and most meaningful things in your life.

6. Something is better than nothing

It's much easier to move an object in motion than an object at rest.

Unless, of course, you want to challenge Sir Isaac freakin' Newton.

Sometimes the most critical thing you can do to sustain a project is to simply keep the balls in the air. This means not giving up during those periods when you can't do something 110%.

Ultra-achievers, like you, have the hardest time embracing this concept. When I first introduce this conversation it's like I'm speaking hieroglyphics.

Since you're so used to doing everything 110%, the thought of 80%, 50% or even 25% ignites all sorts of inner dialogue along the lines of "unacceptable, you're not doing enough, not good enough!"

That's where your ultra-achieving you will either get back to 110%, or abandon ship altogether because you can't handle the self-inflicted guilt.

While I admire you striving to be your best at all times, if you're playing big enough games in your life, you simply won't win every single game. You're not supposed to. You're supposed to win the BIG games.

Roger Federer loses games and sets all the time. Yet he has 18 grand-slam titles. Those are the BIG games you want to win.

The reality is, when you're making big changes in your life, you're swimming against the stream. At the early stages of transformation, 95% of your automatic patterning is working against you. Inevitably you're going to get washed back a few times.

In a former life, if I didn't plan my day to fit in a full 20-minute meditation and 60-minute workout, I would abandon both altogether. If my schedule got hairy and a few of those days happened in succession, I'd find myself completely off the wagon. Getting back on was a bitch.

The present-day version of me realizes that a ten-minute meditation session and a 20-minute workout is better than 0 and 0. I stay in motion.

Remember, it's much easier to stay in motion while you're still in motion.

7. Relentlessly accumulate small wins

How did Andy Dufresne from *Shawshank Redemption* escape from prison? By chiseling no more than spoonfuls of cement, rock and dirt from his cell wall for years (disguised behind his Raquel Welch poster) until the tunnel was big enough for his epic jailbreak.

"The man who removes a mountain begins by carrying away small stones."

- CHINESE PROVERB

From the outside, what may appear to be Herculean efforts are nothing more than a consistent series of small wins. Andy Dufresne was the model of relentlessness in his consistency of accumulating those micro wins – one spoonful at a time.

The reason why small wins are so important is because they eventually catalyze a tipping point, just like the proverbial straw that broke the camel's back. Your success in sustaining your 90-day plan or your efforts in support of your legacy vision hinge on your relentless pursuit of those wins.

Your rituals and habits play a major role in facilitating those wins.

For example, the idea of writing a book is incomprehensible and overwhelming for most people. But it's not as hard as you might think.

Say you want to get really ambitious and write a book in 90 days. Implement a ritual of waking at 5:00am and write 500 words, a modest goal. I'll even let you take weekends off, so you're down to writing 64 days.

At the end of 90 days you'll have 32,000 words, a legitimate-sized book (and longer than this one!)

Mark Twain advises, "The secret of getting started is breaking your complex overwhelming tasks into small manageable tasks and then starting on the first one."

Complete the first task, and then the second. Rinse and repeat your way to extraordinary results through the relentless accumulation of small wins.

WHAT NEXT?

There's a scene in the movie *The Firm* that lasts all of 13 seconds, but it's stuck with me for the 20-plus years since I'd first seen it.

Mitch McDeere (played by Tom Cruise) and Wayne Terrance (Ed Harris) are at a dog track about to watch a race. The scene starts with the hounds shooting out of the gates, ferociously chasing a mechanical bone that glides around the inside of the track. No matter how fast the dogs run, the bone is always just a few feet out of reach.

Mitch: "Doesn't a dog ever get the bone?"

Wayne: "Yeah here it happens once in a while. It's a disaster. They can never get that dog to run again."

I remember feeling like one of those dogs in 2009. I'd finally gotten the bone I'd been chasing my entire life – the riches, the titles, the prestige. And then I just didn't feel like running anymore. I bet you've felt the same way at some point about something in your life as well. Maybe you feel that way now.

That's because you've been chasing the wrong bone.

By now you've come to realize that your pursuit of a future you can't wait to live into can't be attached to something outside yourself (the metaphorical dog chasing the bone.) Instead, the quality of the external world you design is 100% a product of the internal world you've curated. The seeds of your internal beliefs and stories sprout your external behaviors and worldview.

The exciting thing about the fact that 95% of your thoughts, feelings and behaviors are unconscious is the knowing that there will always be something new to discover about yourself. No matter how much you uncover, there will always be more treasure to seek and find. These discoveries lead to a lifetime of growth, adventure and ultimately meaning.

Hell yes.

The ADD Cycle we have just walked through in this book is a process that should be repeated and not a one-time exercise.

---

very new awakening instigates the process to designing a new and intentional way of being. Inevitably these will lead to new and deeper levels of awakenings. The cycle continues.

It's just like any other meaningful practice in your life: eating healthy, working out, playing an instrument, creating art, professional development, spiritual development ... you must keep revisiting, practicing and evolving to continue growing.

That's why I've written this book for you to keep coming back to at different stages of your life. Each time you revisit the Awakening, Disrupting and Designing Cycle, you will view it through a different lens based on that particular time of your life.

Any time you feel you are drifting in an area of your life, that's a sign to pick this book up, thumb through the chapters and take back command of your life.

I had dinner with a friend, Sheena, who recently transformed her life, having lost at least 50 pounds and, more importantly, maintained a healthy weight for 18 months. Not only does she look great, but also her confidence has skyrocketed and she's building on this success by tackling other areas of self-improvement as well – mindset, exercise, professional development.

Her energy is infectious. Everyone around her now feeds off her success – including her husband. He was so inspired by her transformation that he's currently working on dramatically improving his health as well.

Sheena said she'd uncovered so many blind spots – limiting beliefs and stories that were driving her self-defeating behaviors – that despite all her wins, she wondered if she'd only just scratched the surface. "I wonder if I'll ever truly understand everything about why I do what I do?"

My quick answer was, "Hell no you won't."

I *love* believing that we'll never have all the answers. I love knowing that until the day we die we'll be uncovering new treasures as a result of being relentless learners.

The day we "figure everything out," will be the day we catch the bone.

I sure as hell won't ever stop running.

Neither will you.

It is now your time to design the future that you can't wait to live into.

You deserve this. The most important people in your life deserve this.

Take command. Take that first step.

I am here, rooting for you.

– Dominick

RESOURCES

AWAKENING

Books to initiate intentional awakenings:

The Alchemist – Paulo Coelho

Awareness: The Key to Living in Balance – Osho

An Open Heart: Practicing Compassion in Everyday Life
– The Dalai Lama

Buddhism Without Beliefs: A Contemporary Guide to
Awakening – Stephen Batchelor

Fear: Essential Wisdom for Getting Through the Storm
– Thich Nhat Hanh

Lean In: Women, Work and the Will to Lead
– Sheryl Sandberg

Outwitting the Devil: The Secret to Freedom and Success –
Napoleon Hill

The Power of Habit: Why We Do What We Do in Life and
Business – Charles Duhigg

The Power of Now: A Guide to Spiritual Enlightenment
– Eckhart Tolle

Thinking, Fast and Slow – Daniel Kahneman

Sacred Hoops: Spiritual Lessons of a Hardwood Warrior
– Phil Jackson

Siddhartha – Hermann Hesse

*The Way of the Superior Man: A Spiritual Guide to
Mastering the Challenges of Women, Work and Sexual
Desire* – David Deida

Meditation help:

Headspace App (to build a daily practice with
accountability and reminders)

Cory Muscara, The Long Island Center for Mindfulness
(www.LiMindulfnessAndCoaching.com)

Emily Fletcher, Ziva Meditation (search "Emily Fletcher"
on YouTube for her channel)

The Honest Guys (search "The Honest Guys" on YouTube
for excellent guided meditations)

TED Talks:

Make Creative Destruction a Regular Part of Your Routine – Jason Fried (this is a 99U talk, not a TED talk)

The Surprising Habits of Original Thinkers – Adam Grant

What Makes a Good Life? Lessons From the Longest Study on Happiness – Robert Waldinger

---

DISRUPTING

Books to disrupt yourself:

Boundaries: When to Say Yes, How to Say No to Take Control of Your Life – Dr. Henry Cloud

Daring Greatly: How the Courage to be Vulnerable Transforms the Way We Live, Love, Parent and Lead – Brene Brown

Essentialism: The Disciplined of Less – Greg McKeown

The 4-Hour Workweek: Escape 9-5, Live Anywhere, and Join the New Rich – Tim Ferriss

Getting Unstuck: Break Free from the Plateau Effect
– Bob Sullivan and Hugh Thompson

Necessary Endings: The Employees, Businesses and Relationships That We All Have to Give Up In Order to Move Forward – Dr. Henry Cloud

The Life-Changing Magic of Tidying Up: The Japanese Art of Decluttering and Organizing – Marie Kondo

Walden – Henry David Thoreau

TED Talks:

Distracted? Let's Make Technology That Helps Us Spend Our Time Well – Tristan Harris

---

DESIGNING

Books to *design a future you can't wait to live into:*

Big Magic: Creative Living Beyond Fear – Elizabeth Gilbert

Bold: How to Go Big, Create Wealth and Impact the World
– Peter Diamandis and Steven Kotler

Flow: The Psychology of Optimal Experience
– Mihaly Csikszentmihalyi

The Last Safe Investment: Spending Now to Increase Your True Wealth Forever – Bryan Franklin

Mindset: The New Psychology of Success – Carol Dweck

The ONE Thing: The Surprisingly Simple Truth Behind Extraordinary Results – Gary Keller

The Only Way to Win: How Building Higher Character Drives Achievement and Greater Fulfillment in Business and Life – Dr. Jim Loehr

The Rise of Superman: Decoding the Science of Ultimate Human Performance – Steven Kotler

The 12-Week Year: Get More Done in 12 Weeks Than Others Do in 12 Months – Brian P. Moran

Think and Grow Rich – Napoleon Hill

Tools of Titans: The Tactics, Routines and Habits of Billionaires, Icons and World-Class Performers – Tim Ferriss

Two Awesome Hours: Science-Based Strategies to Harness Your Best Time and Get Your Most Important Work Done – Dr Josh Davis

The War of Art: Break Through the Blocks and Win Your Inner Creative Battles – Steven Pressfield

TED Talks:

Bring the Honeymoon Phase Back into Your Relationship – Jon Butcher

How to Gain Control of Your Free Time – Laura Vanderkam

How to Make Work-Life Balance Work – Nigel Marsh

The Psychology of Your Future Self – Dan Gilbert

Should You Live for Your Resume ... or Your Eulogy? – David Brooks

What I Learned from 2,000 Obituaries – Lux Narayan

ABOUT THE AUTHOR

Dominick Quartuccio's passion is helping people design a future they can't wait to live in.

He once had it all – a so-called successful life and lucrative 15-year career in financial services, running sales teams in Fortune 100 companies. He led "a good life."

The result? He was bored, restless and uninspired.

So he left the corporate world and became a human guinea pig, subjecting himself to experiments and experiences that challenged him to assess his long-held beliefs and stories.

Gradually, his behavior changed, and his life changed – for the better.

Dominick is now a mentor, speaker, trainer and author dedicated to supporting others to be better versions of themselves.

He helps successful, stressed and incredibly busy professionals take command of their habits – time, energy, focus and execution – so they can raise their performance in business and all aspects of their day-to-day lives.

When he's not writing, speaking or coaching, he can be found devouring books, meditating, doing a push-up challenge or on an airplane (sometimes where he does all of these things).

DESIGN YOUR FUTURE AT:
DominickQ.com

YOUTUBE:
www.youtube.com/dominickql

FACEBOOK:
www.facebook.com/DominickQuartuccioJr

LINKEDIN:
www.linkedin.com/in/quartuccio/

THE BOOK:
www.dominickq.com/book-design-future/

LET'S CONNECT

There's nothing I love more than working with people who are 110% committed to taking action in designing their future. If this is you, then here are the best ways to get in touch and/or stay connected with me.

GROUP TRAINING AND KEYNOTE SPEAKING

I've had the opportunity to bring this work to some of the largest corporations as well as some of the most exciting emerging businesses and entrepreneurial teams. If you want to explore the possibility of group training or keynote speaking, I'd love to hear from you.

ONE-ON-ONE MENTORING

I take on a select number of clients in a mentoring capacity. I love working with men and women who are committed to massive personal transformation over an extended period of time. If this is you, let's talk.

MEN'S RETREATS

I've been running men's groups and retreats for years now. Given the nonstop busy lives most successful men lead, they often lack a community of strong, ambitious and supportive people around them. That's why I've built a brotherhood of men who come together periodically to immerse themselves in a group experience focused on building bonds and designing their future. If you're interested in knowing when these occur, sign up for my weekly newsletter.

MY WEEKLY NEWSLETTER

Keep current on how to design your future as well as announcements for retreats, webinars, podcasts and videos. Sign up online.

---

dominick@dominickq.com
dominickq.com